Table of Contents

Introduction

What Is Close Reading?

Rigorous standards for English Language Arts place new demands on students and teachers. Students are expected to read and comprehend complex literary and informational texts independently and proficiently. One way to achieve this level of text comprehension is through close reading. Close reading features repeated readings of a text with each reading focused on a specific aspect of the text, for instance, vocabulary or text structure. Through the close reading process, students build up their understanding gradually, so by the end they have a thorough understanding of what they read.

What Is Conquer Close Reading?

Conquer Close Reading is a series of reproducible books for Grades 2–6 that helps students learn to engage in a close reading of a text so that over time they can successfully understand, analyze, and evaluate the ideas in complex texts independently. Students first build close reading skills and then practice and apply them so they develop and hone the skills and abilities necessary to comprehend the increasingly complex texts they will encounter.

In Conquer Close Reading, students learn to unlock the meaning of text by:

- Reading and annotating passages in a variety of genres
- Engaging in close readings and collaborative conversations about the texts
- Examining the vocabulary authors use
- Analyzing text structure of both literary and informational texts
- Evaluating the "big ideas" proposed in texts
- Writing about what they've read and discussed using text evidence

Teaching the Building Block Mini-Lessons

Each grade of Conquer Close Reading begins with two sample texts—one literary and one informational—and a series of twelve mini-lessons. The mini-lessons use the passages to build the skills students need to read closely for deep meaning.

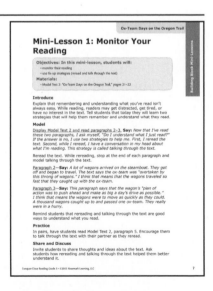

Teaching the Main Passages and Lessons

Each of the fourteen main lessons in Conquer Close Reading features a passage—either literary or informational—that students read and reread to practice and apply the close reading skills they've acquired during instruction of the mini-lessons.

As you start instruction using Conquer Close Reading, keep in mind that students need the opportunity to grapple with the ideas they find in text. They should read the passages independently the first time. Avoid front-loading information or pre-teaching vocabulary. This will allow students to first notice what is confusing so they develop a habit they can use when they read on their own.

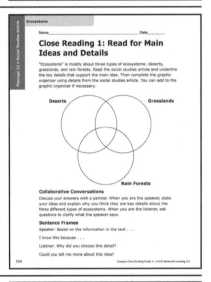

Step 1

The first reading focuses on gaining a general understanding of the text. The students summarize what they read by identifying what the text is mostly about. They also identify key details necessary for understanding. The first reading culminates in a collaborative conversation, giving students an opportunity to build speaking and listening skills, broaden their point of view, and build vocabulary as they compare their impressions of the text and prepare to delve into it in greater detail.

Step 2

The second reading starts the building of a deeper understanding of the text. This reading focuses on four to six vocabulary words: Tier 2 words, challenging words, or examples of figurative language. Students use context to determine word meaning, the connotation in the text, and why the author chose the word.

Step 3

The third reading centers on text structure. For informational texts, one of the five basic patterns of text structure is explored, giving students an opportunity to explore the relationship between meaning and text structure. For literary texts, the focus is on how basic story elements interact to bring life to a work of fiction.

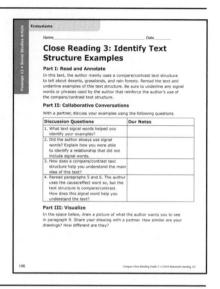

Step 4

The fourth reading focuses directly on the deeper meaning of text. Students make inferences, draw conclusions, and synthesize what a text tells them; consider the broader implications of textual information; and consider the author's purpose and point of view.

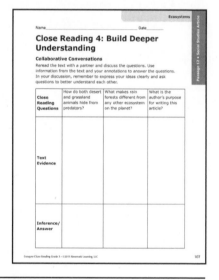

Step 5

Finally, students have an opportunity to write about what they've read. First they analyze a writing prompt based on the text so they know exactly what is expected in their written response. Then they use their annotations, discussion notes, and text evidence as they write a narrative, informative/explanatory, or opinion/argument piece in response to the prompt.

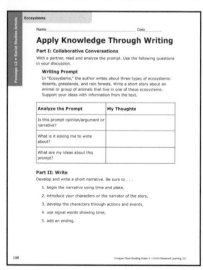

Using the Bonus Tools and Resources

Sentence Resource

The end of each grade-level volume of Conquer Close Reading features resources for students and teachers alike. There is a page of additional sentence frames that students can use during their collaborative conversations.

Writing Checklists

Following the sentence frames are three writing checklists—one each for narrative writing, informative/explanatory writing, and opinion/argument writing. The checklists can be used by students to check their own writing or to conduct peer evaluation. Teachers can also use the checklists to monitor students' progress in developing writing skills.

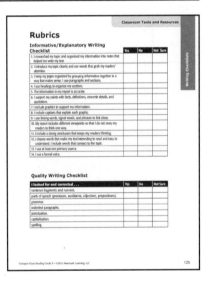

Building Block Mini-Lessons with Model Texts

Mini-Lesson 1: Monitor Your Reading

Objectives: In this mini-lesson, students will:
- monitor their reading
- use fix-up strategies (reread and talk through the text)

Materials:
- Model Text 2: "Ox-Team Days on the Oregon Trail," pages 21–22

Introduce

Explain that remembering and understanding what you've read isn't always easy. While reading, readers may get distracted, get tired, or have no interest in the text. Tell students that today they will learn two strategies that will help them remember and understand what they read.

Model

Display Model Text 2 and read paragraphs 2–3. **Say:** *Now that I've read these two paragraphs, I ask myself, "Do I understand what I just read?" If the answer is no, I use two strategies to help me. First, I reread the text. Second, while I reread, I have a conversation in my head about what I'm reading. This strategy is called talking through the text.*

Reread the text. While rereading, stop at the end of each paragraph and model talking through the text.

Paragraph 2—**Say:** *A lot of wagons arrived on the steamboat. They got off and began to travel. The text says the ox-team was "overtaken by this throng of wagons." I think that means that the wagons traveled so fast that they caught up with the ox-team.*

Paragraph 3—**Say:** *This paragraph says that the wagon's "plan of action was to push ahead and make as big a day's drive as possible." I think that means the wagons were to move as quickly as they could. A thousand wagons caught up to and passed one ox-team. They really were in a hurry.*

Remind students that rereading and talking through the text are good ways to understand what you read.

Practice

In pairs, have students read Model Text 2, paragraph 5. Encourage them to talk through the text with their partner as they reread.

Share and Discuss

Invite students to share thoughts and ideas about the text. Ask students how rereading and talking through the text helped them better understand it.

Mini-Lesson 2: Identify and Annotate Key Details and Main Ideas

Objectives: In this mini-lesson, students will:

- identify key details
- determine main ideas

Materials:

- Model Text 2: "Ox-Team Days on the Oregon Trail," pages 21–22

Introduce

Remind students that texts are made up of details and main ideas. Readers determine main ideas by identifying key details and thinking about how they are connected. Tell students that today they will learn to identify and annotate key details so they can determine a main idea.

Model

Display Model Text 2 and read paragraph 2. **Say:** *Now that I've read this paragraph, I ask myself, "What is the main idea? What details support the main idea?" Watch me as I analyze and annotate the text to answer my questions.*

Reread paragraph 2. After rereading, identify and annotate key details to determine main ideas.

Say: *The first sentence is not that important, but the second and third sentences are. These sentences suggest that a lot of people were moving at one time. I'll highlight those sentences and jot down the main idea.* Model highlighting the text and writing this main idea by the side of paragraph 2.

Say: *The fourth and fifth sentences are also important. They tell me that the travelers were moving fast and were not easy to deal with. This tells me that they must have been in a hurry.* Model highlighting the text and writing the second main idea by the side of paragraph 2. **Say:** *Notice that this paragraph includes two main ideas.*

Practice

In pairs, have students read Model Text 2, paragraph 3. Encourage partners to identify and annotate key details and use them to determine one or more main ideas.

Share and Discuss

Invite students to share thoughts about the text. Ask students how they identified and annotated key details and determined main ideas.

Mini-Lesson 3: Annotate and Analyze Story Characters

Objectives: In this mini-lesson, students will:
- annotate important information about main characters
- use text to analyze main characters

Materials:
- Model Text 1: "Giving," pages 19–20

Introduce

Remind students that readers analyze story characters by thinking about what they say and do as well as how they react to events. Tell students that today they will learn to annotate important information about characters so they can analyze them.

Model

Display Model Text 1 and read paragraphs 2–5. **Say:** *I can tell that this story is about Naomi and her grandfather. But what does this story tell me about them? Watch as I annotate and analyze the text to answer my question.*

Reread paragraphs 2–5. As you reread, annotate the text and analyze the characters.

Say: *I get the idea that Naomi watches what goes on around her. In paragraph 2, she asks Grandpa if he noticed Aunt Emily. Then, in paragraph 4, Naomi tells him that she was watching her. I'll highlight those lines.* Model highlighting those sentences in paragraphs 2 and 4. Draw a line connecting the two paragraphs and write "Naomi observes what goes on around her."

Say: *I get the idea that Grandpa respects Naomi. In paragraph 3, he says he doesn't know why Aunt Emily stopped. Notice that he doesn't tell Naomi to stop talking. In paragraph 5, Grandpa asks Naomi to tell him what Aunt Emily did. He wants to know what Naomi thinks.* Model highlighting sentences in paragraphs 3 and 5. Draw a line connecting the two paragraphs and write "Grandpa respects Naomi's ideas."

Practice

In pairs, have students read paragraphs 6–7. Encourage partners to annotate text that shows how Naomi and Grandpa think differently about Aunt Emily's character.

Share and Discuss

Invite students to share thoughts and ideas about the text. Ask students to explain how they annotated and analyzed Naomi's and Grandpa's descriptions of Aunt Emily.

Mini-Lesson 4: Identify and Annotate Key Words and Phrases

Objectives: In this mini-lesson, students will:
- identify key words and phrases
- identify and annotate context clues that define key words and phrases

Materials:
- Model Text 2: "Ox-Team Days on the Oregon Trail," pages 21–22

Introduce

Remind students that it is often possible to determine the meaning of an unfamiliar word by using the words and sentences around it. This is called using context clues. Tell students that today they will learn how to identify and annotate context clues to define unfamiliar words.

Model

Display Model Text 2 and read paragraph 2. **Say:** *I'm familiar with every word except* **throng**. *I think this word might be important, so watch as I model how to identify context clues that help me define that word.*

Reread paragraph 2. After reading, identify and annotate context clues that help define the unknown word.

Say: *First, I'll highlight the word* **throng**. *Now I'll look for clues that help me define that word. The second sentence says that a steamer could carry a dozen or more wagons with every trip. I'll highlight that clue. Then it says that a steamer made a dozen trips a day and that many more at night. I'll highlight those two clues. That's twenty-four trips a day with twelve wagons on each trip. That's a lot of wagons! I think the word* **throng** *must be another word for "a huge amount." I'll write my definition to the side of the word. This word is important. The huge number of wagons is a key detail in this text.*

Remind students that identifying and annotating context clues will help define words they don't understand.

Practice

In pairs, have students read Model Text 2, paragraph 5. Encourage students to identify and annotate context clues that help them define the word *ills*.

Share and Discuss

Invite students to share thoughts and ideas about the text. Ask students to explain how they identified and annotated context clues that helped them define the unknown word.

Mini-Lesson 5: Group Paragraphs into Meaningful Chunks

Objectives: In this mini-lesson, students will:
- group paragraphs into meaningful chunks
- annotate main ideas

Materials:
- Model Text 1: "Giving," pages 19–20

Introduce

Remind students that stories are made up of main ideas. To identify main ideas, readers must group details and then identify what they have in common. Then readers can put the main ideas together to write a summary. Tell students that today they will learn how to group details together and annotate main ideas.

Model

Display Model Text 1. **Say:** *I notice that this story has many paragraphs. I don't need to find a main idea for each paragraph. I need to group paragraphs that talk about the same thing. I'll call each group a chunk. Then I can identify the main idea for the chunk. Follow along as I read the story aloud.* Read the entire text aloud.

After reading, explain that the first paragraph identifies the main characters: Naomi and Grandpa. Circle the names. Explain that paragraph 2 is a part of this chunk because Naomi answers Grandpa's question. Reread paragraphs 3–6. Explain that these paragraphs belong in this chunk because the two continue to talk about Naomi watching Aunt Emily.

Reread paragraph 7. **Say:** *Ahhh! This one is different. Now Grandpa is telling us about what Emily is like. So the first chunk is from paragraph 1 to paragraph 6.* Bracket paragraphs 1–6 and annotate the main idea. Help students understand the main idea of the first chunk: Aunt Emily doesn't have a lot of money, so her $50 donation confuses Naomi.

Practice

In pairs, have students reread paragraphs 7–13. Encourage students to identify two meaningful chunks of text and annotate main ideas for both. For pairs that struggle, point out the time shift between paragraphs 11 and 12.

Share and Discuss

Invite students to share thoughts and ideas about the text. Ask students to explain how they identified and annotated the remaining chunks.

Building Block Mini-Lessons

Mini-Lesson 6: Annotate and Determine Text Structure and Organization

Objectives: In this mini-lesson, students will:
- deconstruct a descriptive text structure and organization
- annotate a descriptive text structure and organization

Materials:
- Model Text 2: "Ox-Team Days on the Oregon Trail," pages 21–22

Introduce

Explain to students that authors organize their writing in different ways. These are called text structures. It is easier to understand the text if we understand how it is structured and organized. Tell students that today they will learn how to take apart and analyze a descriptive text structure.

Model

Display Model Text 2 and read paragraphs 1–2. **Say:** *I can tell that the author is using mostly descriptive text structure in these paragraphs. This means that the author is making clear images that we can picture as we read. Watch as I model how I know.*

Reread paragraph 1 and **say:** *In the first sentence, the author tells when and where the events took place. I'll highlight the when and where and annotate this information to the side of paragraph 1. In the second sentence, the author describes more about the location. I'll highlight and annotate that to the side of paragraph 1, too.* Model highlighting and annotating the setting.

Reread paragraph 2 and **say:** *In this paragraph, the author describes the steamer, but he doesn't describe what it looks like. He describes what it does. He describes how many wagons it can carry and how many trips it makes each day. I'll highlight and annotate this information. The descriptions in both paragraphs create pictures in my head that help me understand the text.* Model highlighting and annotating the descriptions.

Practice

In pairs, have students read Model Text 2, paragraphs 6 and 7. Encourage students to identify and annotate examples of descriptive text structure. Then ask students to draw a picture of what the descriptions look like to them.

Share and Discuss

Invite students to share their thoughts and ideas about the text. Ask students to explain how they identified and annotated examples of descriptive text structures. Then ask students to share their pictures.

Mini-Lesson 7: Analyze Opinion/ Argument Prompts

Objectives: In this mini-lesson, students will:
- read and analyze an opinion/argument prompt

Materials:
- Mini-Lesson Resources, Opinion/Argument Prompts 1 and 2, page 23

Introduce

Explain that remembering and understanding text isn't always easy. Tell students that today they will learn two strategies that will help them remember and understand what they read.

Model

Display and read aloud Opinion/Argument Prompt 1. **Say:** *Now that I've read the prompt for the first time, I need to make sure I understand the vocabulary and content words. For example, the word* **load** *means "the things they carried in their wagons."*

Next, reread each sentence of the prompt. **Say:** *The first sentence explains the topic. I will be writing about mistakes made by the settlers in "Ox-Team Days on the Oregon Trail." The second sentence tells me exactly what I'm to write about. I'm asked to think about two mistakes the settlers made and to pick which one caused the most problems. So I give my opinion. The last sentence tells me that I need to use information, or evidence, from the text to support my opinion.*

Remind students that analyzing a prompt will help them write a strong essay that answers the question.

Practice

In pairs, have students read Opinion/Argument Prompt 2. Encourage students to analyze the prompt.

Share and Discuss

Invite students to share their thoughts and ideas about the prompt. Ask students to explain how they analyzed the prompt.

Mini-Lesson 8: Analyze Informative/Explanatory Prompts

> **Objectives: In this mini-lesson, students will:**
> • read and analyze an informative/explanatory prompt
>
> **Materials:**
> • Mini-Lesson Resources, Informative/Explanatory Prompts 1 and 2, page 23

Introduce

Explain to students that a prompt is a way to ask a question. Some prompts ask us to provide information or explain something. Tell students that today they will learn how to analyze an informative/explanatory prompt to better answer the question.

Model

Display and read aloud Informative/Explanatory Prompt 1. **Say:** *Now that I've read the prompt for the first time, I need to make sure I understand the vocabulary and content words. For example, the word **compare** tells me that I'm going to look at how two things are the same and how they are different. Another important word is **handled**. This word means "take care of" or "deal with."*

Next, reread each sentence of the prompt. **Say:** *The first sentence explains the topic. I will write about the beginning and ending parts of the trip taken by the settlers in "Ox-Team Days on the Oregon Trail." The second sentence tells me exactly what I'm to write about. I'm asked to compare the part of the trip at the beginning of the text with the part of the trip at the end of the text. So I'm giving an explanation. The third sentence tells me what to compare. I need to compare not only the events of the trip, but also how the settlers handled, or dealt with, the events. The last sentence tells me that I need to use information, or evidence, from the text to support my explanation.*

Remind students that analyzing a prompt will help them write a strong essay that answers the question.

Practice

In pairs, have students read Informative/Explanatory Prompt 2. Encourage students to analyze the prompt.

Share and Discuss

Invite students to share their thoughts and ideas about the prompt. Ask students to explain how they analyzed the prompt.

Mini-Lesson 9: Analyze Narrative Prompts

> **Objectives: In this mini-lesson, students will:**
> • read and analyze a narrative prompt
>
> **Materials:**
> • Mini-Lesson Resources, Narrative Prompts 1 and 2, page 23

Introduce

Explain to students that a prompt is a way to ask a question. Some prompts ask us to write a short story or other fiction piece. Tell students that today they will learn how to analyze a narrative prompt to better answer the question.

Model

Display and read aloud Narrative Prompt 1. **Say:** *Now that I've read the prompt for the first time, I need to make sure I understand the vocabulary and content words. For example, the word **charity** means "giving to those who have less than you."*

Next, reread each sentence of the prompt. **Say:** *The first two sentences explain the topic. I'll write a story about Aunt Emily donating money to charity. The third sentence tells me how I'm to write the story. I need to write in the first person. So I'll use the word **I** as if I were Aunt Emily. The last two sentences tell me what to include in my story. I need to explain how I, or Aunt Emily, came to have $50 extra. That's a good one. I can think of lots of ways. Maybe I found the money on the ground. Maybe I babysat the neighbors' children. Finally, I need to use words that describe Aunt Emily's character. Grandpa says that she'll save food off her own plate to feed stray cats. That must mean that she thinks about others before herself.*

Remind students that analyzing a prompt will help them write a strong short story that answers the question.

Practice

In pairs, have students read Narrative Prompt 2. Encourage students to analyze the prompt.

Share and Discuss

Invite students to share their thoughts and ideas about the prompt. Ask students to explain how they analyzed the prompt.

Mini-Lesson 10: Choose Text Evidence That Supports the Prompt

Objectives: In this mini-lesson, students will:

• identify text evidence that supports the writer's answer to a prompt

Materials:

• Model Text 2: "Ox-Team Days on the Oregon Trail," pages 21–22
• Mini-Lessons Resources, Informative/Explanatory Prompt 2, page 23
• Mini-Lessons Resources, Opinion/Argument Prompt 2, page 23

Introduce

Explain to students that when they are writing to a prompt, they must include evidence from the text that supports their answer. Tell students that today they will learn how to identify text evidence that best supports their ideas.

Model

Display and read Informative/Explanatory Prompt 2. **Say:** *I understand what I am supposed to do. Now I need to review the text, decide what I think, and identify text evidence that supports what I think.*

Read paragraphs 1–5 of "Ox-Team Days on the Oregon Trail." Explain that these paragraphs do not help answer the prompt because they do not discuss what the settlers abandoned. Read paragraphs 6 and 7. As you read, annotate the paragraphs. **Say:** *After reading these paragraphs, I can see that the settlers used common sense to determine when to abandon their items. It seems like the first items, such as a stove or a bed, were large and heavy. They put too much weight on the wagon and slowed it down. Next, settlers gave away comfy things like blankets and quilts. It was more important to keep things they needed to survive, such as food. Even if they had to give up their wagon, at least they could eat. Finally, though, they had to give up their food, too. Now what were they to do?*

Remind students that identifying text evidence that answers the prompt will help them write a strong essay.

Practice

In pairs, have students read Opinion/Argument Prompt 2. Encourage students to determine an answer and identify text evidence that supports the answer to the prompt. (Evidence should come from paragraphs 6 and 7.)

Share and Discuss

Invite students to share their thoughts and ideas. Ask students to explain how they identified text evidence to support the answer to the prompt.

Mini-Lesson 11: Collaborative Conversations: Speakers Express Ideas Clearly

Objectives: In this mini-lesson, students will:
- provide concise and understandable explanations

Materials:
- Model Text 1: "Giving," pages 19–20

Introduce

Remind students that everyone has ideas and wants them to be heard. It is important, however, to make our thoughts clear and easy to understand when we speak. Tell students that today they will learn how to express ideas clearly when they speak.

Model

Display Model Text 1. Read paragraphs 7–11. **Say:** *I think these paragraphs show that Naomi believes that money is the only thing you can give. I'll write that along the side of the paragraphs. I think this because Naomi says she's never given because she doesn't have fifty dollars. When Grandpa answers, "Sometimes you just give what you can," Naomi does not know what he is talking about.* Model highlighting these lines.

Say: *Notice how I came up with my thought and wrote it down. Next, I highlighted the evidence in the story that supported my idea. When it's my turn to speak, I'll share my thought first and then use the evidence from the text to show how I came up with that thought. Because my thoughts will be clearly organized, my listeners will understand me.*

Practice

In pairs, have students read Model Text 1, paragraphs 12 and 13. Encourage students to answer the following question using evidence from the text. Have pairs practice expressing their thoughts and evidence in a clear way.

> Going to the nursing home was a good activity for Naomi because she learned a valuable lesson about giving. How was this activity good for Grandpa? Use evidence from the text to support your answer.

Share and Discuss

Invite students to share answers and text evidence. Ask students to explain what they learned from this activity about clearly expressing their ideas.

Mini-Lesson 12: Collaborative Conversations: Listeners Ask Thoughtful Questions

Objectives: In this mini-lesson, students will:
- ask questions to understand

Materials:
- Model Text 1: "Giving," pages 19–20
- Mini-Lesson Resources, Ask Questions Anchor Chart, page 23

Introduce

Remind students that it isn't always easy to understand what someone is saying. Sometimes, speakers are not as clear as they could be. Sometimes, we just have trouble understanding the topic. Tell students that today they will ask questions to help them understand what is being said.

Model

Display Model Text 1. Read paragraphs 7–11. **Say:** *Pretend I am the speaker. I'm going to tell you what I think about these paragraphs. I think Grandpa cares about Naomi. Now pretend that I am the listener. I'm confused. Why does the speaker think this? What information from the story makes her think this way? When you are confused, ask questions. Here are some questions or phrases that you can use when you don't understand what the speaker is saying.*

Display the Ask Questions Anchor Chart. Invite students to follow along as you read the questions. Tell students to ask one or more of these questions if they are confused. Invite a student to ask you one of these questions. **Say:** *Oh, yes. I didn't make myself clear. I think this way because Grandpa is taking the time to help Naomi learn this valuable lesson. He asks her questions and then comes up with a plan to help her learn.* Remind students to ask questions when they don't understand what is being said.

Practice

Read paragraphs 9–11. Tell students that these paragraphs lead you to think that Naomi does not believe she will learn anything new from Grandpa. In pairs, have students consider what questions they might ask to understand why you think this.

Share and Discuss

Invite students to share their questions. Provide text evidence to answer their questions. (Possible text evidence: "Like what, then?"; "She gave him a skeptical look and shrugged.")

Name_____ Date_____

Model Text 1: Realistic Fiction
Giving

by Joshua E. Keeler

1   The kitchen smelled of bananas. Naomi stopped stirring her bowl of batter and looked out the apartment window at the park across the street. Her eyebrows were scrunched, and she was biting her lip. Grandpa closed the oven door, wiped his forehead with the back of his hand, and said, "What are you thinking about over there, Naomi?"

2   Looking up from the window, she paused for a second before speaking. "When we were in the park earlier, did you notice what Aunt Emily did when she let us walk ahead?"

3   He tapped his pointy chin with his finger. "I do remember that she stopped, but I didn't see why."

4   Naomi looked around and whispered loudly, as if telling a secret, "Well . . . I was watching her."

5   "Ah, a little snoop!" Grandpa joked. He swiped some batter that had dripped onto his apron and wiped it on her nose. "So, what did she do?"

6   Naomi's voice became more excited. "Did you notice the charity table that was asking for money to help buy school clothes for poor children?" Grandpa shook his head. "Well, I saw Aunt Emily give them fifty dollars! Fifty! She can't even afford a television. Practically everything she owns is used."

continued

Model Text 1 • Realistic Fiction

Name_____ Date_____

7   Grandpa smiled and said, "Your aunt has always been like that. When she was your age, she would save scraps from her dinner and feed them to stray cats at night." He sat down across from Naomi at the kitchen table. "I'm sure it's worth it for her. It feels pretty good to give, you know. Have you ever tried?"

8   Naomi looked toward the ceiling and thought. "Not that I can think of. But I don't have fifty dollars to give, Grandpa."

9   "Sometimes you just give what you can."

10   "Like what, then?"

11   Grandpa looked down at the bowl of batter and then back up at Naomi. "Well, I've got an idea, but you've got to be willing to give up our dessert." She gave him a skeptical look and shrugged.

12   For the rest of the afternoon, they mixed, poured, baked, and wrapped warm loaves of banana bread. Then Grandpa and Naomi got on the bus and rode to a retirement center. Before they went inside, Grandpa spied an old woman sitting near the window. "This was your grandmother's good friend," he said. "She's probably pretty lonely, since her children moved far away."

13   As they walked in, the woman's face lit up. They gave her the banana bread, and she thanked them over and over. Grandpa and Naomi sat and talked with her for an hour. Before they left, they promised to come back soon. Naomi was all smiles walking back to the bus stop. "You know, I can see why Aunt Emily likes giving. Seeing that woman happy was much better than eating a few slices of banana bread."

14   Grandpa smiled too. "All that baking made me hungry. What do you say we go out to eat tonight?"

Name_____ Date_____

Model Text 2: Social Studies Article
Ox-Team Days on the Oregon Trail

(adapted excerpt from *Ox-Team Days on the Oregon Trail*, by Ezra Meeker, 1927)

1   We crossed the Missouri River on the 17th and 18th of May. The next day we made a short drive and camped within hearing of the steamboat whistle that sounded far over the prairie.

2   The whistle announced the arrival of a steamer. The steamer could carry a dozen or more wagons across the river at a time. A dozen or more trips could be made during the day, with as many more at night. Very soon we were overtaken by this throng of wagons. They gave us some troubles, and much discomfort.

3   The rush for the West was then at its height. The plan of action was to push ahead and make as big a day's drive as possible. So it is not to be wondered at that nearly all the thousand wagons that crossed the river after we did soon passed us.

4   "Now, just let them rush on. If we keep cool, we'll catch them before long," I told my companions.

continued

Name_____ Date_____

5   And we did. We passed many a team, broken down as a result of those first few days of rush. People often brought these and other ills upon themselves by their own foolishness.

Left on the Trail

6   Many folks did not go far before giving up the heavy loads. Soon we began to see abandoned property. First it might be a table or a cupboard, or perhaps a bed or a cookstove. Then feather beds, blankets, quilts, and pillows were seen. Very soon, here and there would be an abandoned wagon. Then we saw supplies like flour and bacon. All were left.

7   It was a case of help yourself if you would. No one would stop you. In some places a sign was posted: "Help yourself." Hundreds of wagons were left and hundreds of tons of goods. People seemed to vie with one another in giving away their things. There was no chance to sell, and they disliked to destroy their goods.

Mini-Lesson Resources

Opinion/Argument Prompt 1

In "Ox-Team Days on the Oregon Trail," settlers made two important mistakes. They moved too quickly and carried heavy loads in their wagons. After reading the article, write a short essay in which you identify the mistake you think caused more problems for the settlers. Support your opinion with evidence from the text.

Opinion/Argument Prompt 2

In "Ox-Team Days on the Oregon Trail," settlers had to leave many of their possessions behind. After reading the article, write a short essay in which you offer a solution to this problem. Support your opinion with evidence from the text.

Informative/Explanatory Prompt 1

In "Ox-Team Days on the Oregon Trail," the trip began one way and ended another way. After reading the article, write a short essay in which you compare events in paragraphs 1–4 with events in paragraphs 5–7. In your comparison, explain differences in events as well as how the settlers handled these events. Support your writing with evidence from the text.

Informative/Explanatory Prompt 2

In "Ox-Team Days on the Oregon Trail," settlers abandoned much of their property. After reading the article, write a short essay in which you analyze how settlers decided the order of things to abandon. Support your writing with evidence from the text.

Narrative Prompt 1

In "Giving," Naomi watches as her aunt Emily donates $50 to a charity table. After reading the story, write a short narrative about this event from Aunt Emily's point of view. Use the first person *I*. In your story, describe how you think Aunt Emily came to have $50 extra that she could donate. Also, be sure to describe Aunt Emily using evidence from "Giving."

Narrative Prompt 2

In "Giving," Grandpa helps Naomi learn a lesson about charity. After reading the story, write a short narrative in which you tell how Naomi helps a friend learn the same lesson. In your story, describe the friend and the steps Naomi follows to teach the lesson.

Ask Questions Anchor Chart

Questions to Help My Understanding

1. What did you mean when you said _____?
2. Why do you think that way?
3. What evidence from the text makes you think that way?
4. Tell me more about _____.

Close Readings: Main Passages and Lessons

Name_____ Date_____

Passage 1: Mystery • *The Hidden Cottage*

by Kathleen Bush

1   Willa had never much enjoyed visiting her grandfather's farm until she found the hidden cottage.

2   It happened one hot afternoon. Willa had grown bored of helping her grandfather pull weeds out of the strawberry field. There were no paths leading through the woods, but she walked in anyway.

3   She sighed as she pushed her way through bush after prickly bush. She groaned as she swatted away a mosquito. She yelped as she stubbed her toe on a rock. When she looked down at the ground to glare at the rock, she discovered instead a jar. She picked it up to inspect it. The glass was cloudy with age, and the lid was rusty. Inside it were metal nails.

4   As she pushed her way through the next bush, she discovered something even more surprising: a small, white cottage. There were curtains hanging in the little windows. There was also a small porch with two small chairs on it.

5   When Willa walked closer to the cottage, she could see that the white paint on it was peeling and that the porch was covered in cobwebs and fallen leaves. She peered through one of the dirty windows. The house had only one room inside. In the middle of the room was a small, dusty table with two chairs.

6   Willa no longer felt bored!

7   When Willa got back to the farm, she excitedly asked her grandfather about the cottage.

continued

Name_____ Date_____

8   "Marion should be able to tell you all about it," her grandfather said. Marion was the closest neighbor. She had lived on the farm on the other side of the woods her entire life.

9   The next morning, Willa's grandfather drove her over to Marion's farm for lunch.

10   "I have some work to do back at home. I'll pick you up later, Willa," Willa's grandfather explained. He winked at Marion.

11   Willa immediately asked Marion about the cottage in the woods. Marion smiled.

12   "When I was a girl, your grandmother was my best friend. We loved to play in the woods together. My father built that cottage. It was our playhouse," Marion explained. "Your grandmother loved it."

13   When Willa returned to her grandfather's farm that afternoon, she told her grandfather that she was going back to the cottage to explore.

14   "Good idea!" her grandfather said with a wink.

15   When Willa arrived at the cottage, she gasped in surprise. The cottage looked new! The porch was clean, and the walls looked freshly painted. Someone else had been there.

16   Willa found a note attached to the door.

17   It read:

18   Willa,

19   Your grandmother would want you to enjoy the cottage.

20   Love,

21   Your Grandfather

22   Willa smiled.

Name_____ Date_____

Close Reading 1: Read for Story Elements

"The Hidden Cottage" is mostly about a young girl's discovery on her grandfather's farm. Read the mystery and underline the key elements of the story. Then complete the graphic organizer using details from the mystery. You can add to the graphic organizer if necessary.

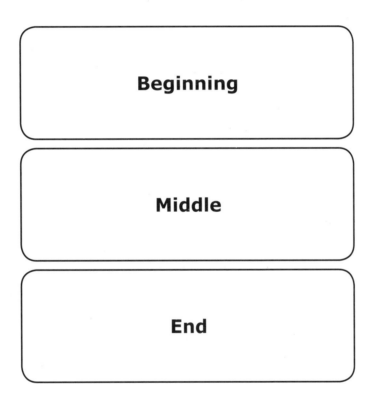

Beginning

Middle

End

Collaborative Conversations

Discuss your answers with a partner. When you are the speaker, state your ideas and explain why you think they are key elements of the story. When you are the listener, ask questions to clarify what the speaker says.

Sentence Frames

Speaker: In the beginning of the story . . .

At the end of the story . . .

Listener: Why did you choose this detail?

Could you tell me more about this idea?

Name_____ Date_____

Close Reading 2: Build Vocabulary

Reread the text. Locate each word or phrase, and identify context clues to determine its meaning. Underline the context clues as you read. Share your definitions or meanings with your partner and check your definitions using a dictionary.

Word or Phrase	Context Clues	What the Text Says It Means
enjoyed		
swatted		
peered		
excitedly		
gasped		

Think-Share-Write

Collaborate with your partner to generate new sentences showing your understanding of each word or phrase. Choose two of the new sentences and write them in the space below.

_____

_____

_____

_____

Name_____ Date_____

Close Reading 3: Identify Text Structure Examples

Part I: Read and Annotate

In this text, the author mainly uses a sequence text structure to tell about a young girl's discovery on her grandfather's farm. Reread the text and underline examples of this text structure. Be sure to underline any signal words or phrases used by the author that reinforce the author's use of the sequence text structure.

Part II: Collaborative Conversations

With a partner, discuss your examples using the following questions.

Discussion Questions	Our Notes
1. What text signal words helped you identify your examples?	
2. Does the author always use signal words? Explain how you were able to identify a relationship that did not include signal words.	
3. How does a sequence text structure help you understand the main idea of this text?	
4. Reread paragraph 3. The author uses descriptive words like *cloudy* and *rusty*, but the text structure is sequence. How do these words help you understand the text?	

Part III: Visualize

Draw a picture of what the author wants you to see in paragraphs 5 and 6. Share your drawing with a partner. How are your drawings similar? How are they different?

Name_____ Date_____

Close Reading 4: Build Deeper Understanding

Collaborative Conversations

Reread the text with a partner and discuss the questions. Use information from the text and your annotations to answer the questions. In your discussion, remember to express your ideas clearly and ask questions to better understand each other.

Close Reading Questions	What problem sets the events of the story in motion?	Why does Willa's grandfather take Willa to Marion's farm for lunch?	What is the author's purpose for writing this mystery?
Text Evidence			
Inference/ Answer			

Name_____ Date_____

Apply Knowledge Through Writing

Part I: Collaborative Conversations

With a partner, read and analyze the prompt. Use the following questions in your discussion.

Writing Prompt

In "The Hidden Cottage," the author writes about a young girl's discovery at her grandfather's farm. Write a short summary of the story. Tell what happens in the beginning, middle, and end of the story.

Analyze the Prompt	My Thoughts
Is this prompt informative/ explanatory or opinion/argument?	
What is it asking me to write about?	
What are my ideas about this prompt?	

Part II: Write

Develop and write a short informative essay. Be sure to . . .

1. state your topic,

2. use details and text evidence to develop the topic,

3. use linking words and phrases,

4. add a concluding sentence.

Name_____ Date_____

Passage 2: Ojibwe Folktale:
Wenebojo and the Cranberries

by Kathleen Bush

1 As Wenebojo walked along the edge of the lake, his hunger increased. And as his hunger became greater, so did his frustration.

2 "I am a demi-god!" he grumbled. "When I am hungry, I deserve to be fed! What will present itself to me to be eaten?"

3 He waited for a response. But no fish jumped out of the lake to be eaten. No birds flew out of the woods to be eaten. He scowled at the woods. He scowled at the lake. He picked up a rock and threw it at the woods. He picked up his feet and stomped them in the shallow water at the edge of the lake, sending the surface into a frenzy.

4 When Wenebojo's stomach growled loudly and reminded him of his hunger, he stopped stomping. As the water settled, he noticed dozens of tiny, red orbs lying below the water's surface nearby.

5 "Cranberries!" Wenebojo shouted with glee. "Juicy cranberries have presented themselves for me to feast upon!"

6 Wenebojo waded over to the cranberries. He eagerly dipped his hand into the water to grab a handful, his mouth watering expectantly. As he pulled his hand back out of the water, his eyes widened with surprise. His hand was empty. The cranberries were still lying in the shallow water!

7 Wenebojo took a deep breath and dipped his face into the water to bite the cranberries. But only water entered his mouth. He spat the water out angrily.

Name_____ Date_____

8   "What trickery is this?" he screeched. "I do not require drink! I require food! Present yourselves to my stomach!"

9   With that, Wenebojo dove headfirst toward the cranberries.

10   "My precious head!" he moaned as he came up for air. He clutched his forehead in his hands and lay down on his back on the shore. All he had found underwater was a sharp rock, against which he had bumped his forehead. His mouth and his stomach were still empty.

11   After a minute, Wenebojo pulled his hands away from his forehead to yell at the cranberries. Instead, he yelled in surprise. Branches of a tree hung over the spot where he was lying, and on every branch there were clusters of juicy, red cranberries!

12   "The cranberries in the water were just a reflection!" he growled. He leapt up and tore every single cranberry off the tree, flinging all of them to the ground.

13   "I am a demi-god!" he grumbled. "When I am hungry, I deserve to be fed!" His stomach rumbled as he walked away.

Name_____ Date_____

Close Reading 1: Read for Story Elements

"Wenebojo and the Cranberries" is mostly about a man named Wenebojo who is mad with hunger. Read the folktale and underline the key events of the story. Then complete the graphic organizer using details from the folktale. You can add to the graphic organizer if necessary.

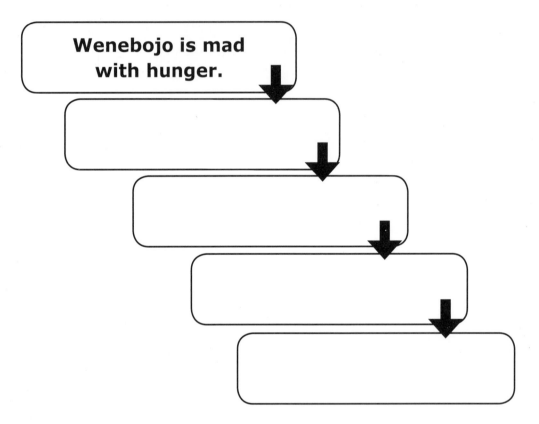

Wenebojo is mad with hunger.

Collaborative Conversations

Discuss your answers with a partner. When you are the speaker, state your ideas and explain why you think they tell about the key events of the story. When you are the listener, ask questions to clarify what the speaker says.

Sentence Frames

Speaker: The most important event in the story . . .

I chose this detail because . . .

Listener: What details does the author use to describe that?

Tell me why you chose this detail.

Name_____ Date_____

Close Reading 2: Build Vocabulary

Reread the text. Locate each word or phrase, and identify context clues to determine its meaning. Underline the context clues as you read. Share your definitions or meanings with your partner and check your definitions using a dictionary.

Word or Phrase	Context Clues	What the Text Says It Means
increased		
deserve		
settled		
dozens		
feast		

Think-Share-Write

Collaborate with your partner to generate new sentences showing your understanding of each word or phrase. Choose two of the new sentences and write them in the space below.

_____

_____

_____

Name_____ Date_____

Close Reading 3: Identify Text Structure Examples

Part I: Read and Annotate

In this text, the author mainly uses a sequence text structure to tell about Wenebojo and what he does when he is mad with hunger. Reread the text and underline examples of this text structure. Be sure to underline any signal words or phrases used by the author that reinforce the author's use of the sequence text structure.

Part II: Collaborative Conversations

With a partner, discuss your examples using the following questions.

Discussion Questions	Our Notes
1. What text signal words helped you identify your examples?	
2. Does the author always use signal words? Explain how you were able to identify the order of events without signal words.	
3. How does a sequence text structure help you understand the main idea of this text?	
4. Reread paragraphs 3 and 4. The author uses descriptive words like *scowled*, *frenzy*, and *below*, but the text structure is sequence. How do these words help you understand the text?	

Part III: Visualize

Draw a picture of what the author wants you to see in paragraphs 11 and 12. Share your drawing with a partner. How are your drawings similar? How are they different?

Name_____ Date_____

Close Reading 4: Build Deeper Understanding

Collaborative Conversations

Reread the text with a partner and discuss the questions. Use information from the text and your annotations to answer the questions. In your discussion, remember to express your ideas clearly and ask questions to better understand each other.

Close Reading Questions	How does Wenebojo respond to his hunger?	What is the moral, or lesson, of this story?	What is the author's purpose for writing this folktale?
Text Evidence			
Inference/ Answer			

Name_____ Date_____

Apply Knowledge Through Writing

Part I: Collaborative Conversations

With a partner, read and analyze the prompt. Use the following questions in your discussion.

Writing Prompt

In "Wenebojo and the Cranberries," the author writes about a man named Wenebojo who is mad with hunger. Write a short story that tells what happens to Wenebojo after he walks away from the cranberries. Support your ideas with key elements from the folktale.

Analyze the Prompt	My Thoughts
Is this prompt opinion/argument or narrative?	
What is it asking me to write about?	
What are my ideas about this prompt?	

Part II: Write

Develop and write a short narrative. Be sure to . . .

1. begin the narrative using time and place,

2. introduce your characters or the narrator of the story,

3. develop the characters through actions and events,

4. use signal words showing time,

5. add an ending.

Name_____ Date_____

Passage 3: Poem
Recuerdo

by Edna St. Vincent Millay

1   We were very tired, we were very merry—

2   We had gone back and forth all night on the ferry.

3   It was bare and bright, and smelled like a stable—

4   But we looked into a fire, we leaned across a table,

5   We lay on a hill-top underneath the moon;

6   And the whistles kept blowing, and the dawn came soon.

7   We were very tired, we were very merry—

8   We had gone back and forth all night on the ferry;

9   And you ate an apple, and I ate a pear,

10 From a dozen of each we had bought somewhere;

11 And the sky went wan, and the wind came cold,

12 And the sun rose dripping, a bucketful of gold.

continued →

Name_____ Date_____

13 We were very tired, we were very merry,

14 We had gone back and forth all night on the ferry.

15 We hailed, "Good morrow, mother!" to a shawl-covered head,

16 And bought a morning paper, which neither of us read;

17 And she wept, "God bless you!" for the apples and pears,

18 And we gave her all our money but our subway fares.

_____
_____
_____
_____
_____
_____
_____
_____
_____
_____
_____
_____
_____
_____
_____
_____

Name_____ Date_____

Close Reading 1: Read for Poetry Elements

"Recuerdo" describes a memorable night that two people share together, riding back and forth on a ferry. Read the poem and underline the words that describe the night. Think about how the author uses sensory details to describe what they see, hear, feel, and smell. Then complete the graphic organizer.

See	Hear	Feel	Smell

Collaborative Conversations

Discuss your answers with a partner. When you are the speaker, state your ideas and explain why you think they help the reader imagine the events of the night. When you are the listener, ask questions to clarify what the speaker says.

Sentence Frames

Speaker: This detail helps me imagine . . .

The author explores the idea that . . .

Listener: Could you tell me more about that detail?

What evidence in the text leads you to say that?

Name_____ Date_____

Close Reading 2: Build Vocabulary

Reread the text. Locate each word or phrase, and identify context clues to determine its meaning. Underline the context clues as you read. Share your definitions or meanings with your partner and check your definitions using a dictionary.

Word or Phrase	Context Clues	What the Text Says It Means
forth		
leaned		
underneath		
dawn		

Think-Share-Write

Collaborate with your partner to generate new sentences showing your understanding of each word or phrase. Choose two of the new sentences and write them in the space below.

_____

_____

_____

_____

Name_____ Date_____

Close Reading 3: Identify Text Structure Examples

Part I: Read and Annotate

In this text, the author mainly uses a descriptive text structure to create images of a memorable night. Reread the text and underline examples of this text structure. Be sure to underline any signal words or phrases used by the author that reinforce the author's use of the descriptive text structure.

Part II: Collaborative Conversations

With a partner, discuss your examples using the following questions.

Discussion Questions	Our Notes
1. What text signal words helped you identify your examples?	
2. Did the author always use signal words? Explain how you were able to identify a relationship that did not include signal words.	
3. How does a descriptive text structure help you understand the main idea of this text?	
4. Underline the last word in each line. The author uses an AABBCC rhyme pattern. How does this pattern affect how the poem sounds?	

Part III: Visualize

Draw a picture of what the author wants you to see in lines 11 and 12. Share your drawing with a partner. How are your drawings similar? How are they different?

Name_____ Date_____

Close Reading 4: Build Deeper Understanding

Collaborative Conversations

Reread the text with a partner and discuss the questions. Use information from the text and your annotations to answer the questions. In your discussion, remember to express your ideas clearly and ask questions to better understand each other.

Close Reading Questions	How much time passes in this poem? How do you know?	How does the author create a happy mood?	What happens at the end of the poem? Why do they characters do this?
Text Evidence			
Inference/ Answer			

Name_____ Date_____

Apply Knowledge Through Writing

Part I: Collaborative Conversations

With a partner, read and analyze the prompt. Use the following questions in your discussion.

Writing Prompt

The author of "Recuerdo" uses sensory details to describe a memorable night with a friend. Write a poem that describes a memorable time with a friend. Use sensory details that describe what you see, hear, feel, and smell.

Analyze the Prompt	My Thoughts
Is this prompt informative/ explanatory or narrative?	
What is it asking me to write about?	
What are my ideas about this prompt?	

Part II: Write

Develop and write a poem. Be sure to . . .

1. describe a memorable time with a friend,

2. use a descriptive text structure,

3. use sensory details, including smell, taste, touch, sound, and sight,

4. use line breaks.

Name_____ Date_____

Passage 4: Fable
The Cobbler and the Rich Man
by Lida Brown McMurry

1   A cobbler worked in his shop from morning until night, and as he worked he sang. Tired people who heard him were rested, and sad men and women were cheered as they came near the shop. Children visited him and watched him at his work and heard him sing. They called him Jolly Gregory.

2   "How can he sing when he works so hard and makes so little?" many asked. But still his singing went on.

3   Across the road from the cobbler lived a rich man. His home was beautiful, his clothes fine, and his fare the best that money could buy. But never in his life had he been known to give to anyone who needed help. He was really poor, for he lacked one thing which he very much wanted— sleep. Sometimes he could not get to sleep until early morning; then his neighbor's song would waken him. He wished that sleep could be bought for money.

4   One day he said to himself, "I believe I will help that cobbler over the way. He has a hard time to make enough money to buy his food and clothes." So he sent for the cobbler.

5   "Jolly Gregory," he said, "how much do you earn in a year?"

6   "How much a year?" replied the cobbler, scratching his head. "I never reckon my money in that way. It goes as fast as it comes, but I am glad to be able to earn it. I cobble on from day to day and earn a living."

Name_____ Date_____

7   "You are a happy man now," said the rich man, "but I will make you happier," and he handed the cobbler five hundred dollars. "Go spend this money carefully. It will supply your needs for many days," he said.

8   The cobbler had never dreamed of so much money before. He thought it was enough to keep him in food and clothes all his life.

9   He took the money home and hid it, but he hid his joy with it. He stopped singing and became sad. He could not sleep for fear of robbers. He thought that everyone who came into his shop was trying to find out his secret, or wished a gift. When a cat ran over the floor, he thought a thief had slipped through the door.

10   At last he could bear it no longer. He took the money, hurried to the rich man, and cried, "Oh, give me back my songs and my sweet sleep! Here is your money, every cent of it. I made a poor trade."

11   The rich man looked at him and said, "I thought I had made you happy. I have not missed your songs, for, strange as it may seem, I have been sleeping soundly ever since I talked with you."

Name_____ Date_____

Close Reading 1: Read for Story Elements

"The Cobbler and the Rich Man" is mostly about a trade between a poor cobbler and a rich man. Read the fable and underline the key elements of the story. Then complete the graphic organizer using details from the fable. You can add to the graphic organizer if necessary.

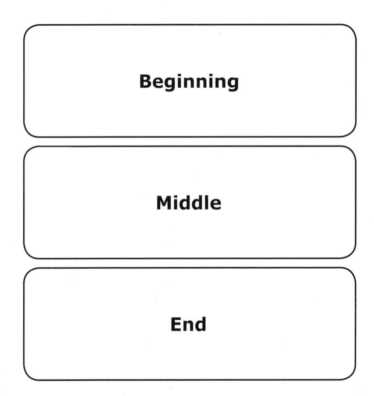

Beginning

Middle

End

Collaborative Conversations

Discuss your answers with a partner. When you are the speaker, state your ideas and explain why you think they describe key elements of the story. When you are the listener, ask questions to clarify what the speaker says.

Sentence Frames

Speaker: In the beginning of the story . . .

At the end of the story . . .

Listener: What details does the author use to describe that?

Why did you choose this detail?

Passage 4 • Fable

Name_____ Date_____

Close Reading 2: Build Vocabulary

Reread the text. Locate each word or phrase, and identify context clues to determine its meaning. Underline the context clues as you read. Share your definitions or meanings with your partner and check your definitions using a dictionary.

Word or Phrase	Context Clues	What the Text Says It Means
lacked		
earn		
bear		
trade		
soundly		

Think-Share-Write

Collaborate with your partner to generate new sentences showing your understanding of each word or phrase. Choose two of the new sentences and write them in the space below.

_____

_____

_____

_____

Name_____ Date_____

Close Reading 3: Identify Text Structure Examples

Part I: Read and Annotate

In this text, the author mainly uses sequence text structure to tell about a trade between a poor cobbler and a rich man. Reread the text and underline examples of this text structure. Be sure to underline any signal words or phrases used by the author that reinforce the author's use of the sequence text structure.

Part II: Collaborative Conversations

With a partner, discuss your examples using the following questions.

Discussion Questions	Our Notes
1. What text signal words helped you identify your examples?	
2. Did the author always use signal words? Explain how you were able to identify a relationship that did not include signal words.	
3. How does a sequence text structure help you understand the main idea of this text?	
4. Reread paragraph 3. The author uses descriptive words like *beautiful* and *fine*, but the text structure is sequence. How do these words help you understand the text?	

Part III: Visualize

Draw a picture of what the author wants you to see in paragraphs 9 and 10. Share your drawing with a partner. How are your drawings similar? How are they different?

Name_____ Date_____

Close Reading 4: Build Deeper Understanding

Collaborative Conversations

Reread the text with a partner and discuss the questions. Use information from the text and your annotations to answer the questions. In your discussion, remember to express your ideas clearly and ask questions to better understand each other.

Close Reading Questions	Why does the rich man give the cobbler money?	Why does the cobbler stop singing?	What is the author's point of view about money?
Text Evidence			
Inference/ Answer			

Name_____ Date_____

Apply Knowledge Through Writing

Part I: Collaborative Conversations

With a partner, read and analyze the prompt. Use the following questions in your discussion.

Writing Prompt

In "The Cobbler and the Rich Man," the author writes about a trade between a poor cobbler and a rich man. Write a short opinion essay that answers the following question: Is it better to be rich or happy? Support your opinion with evidence from the text.

Analyze the Prompt	My Thoughts
Is this prompt informative/ explanatory or opinion/argument?	
What is it asking me to write about?	
What are my ideas about this prompt?	

Part II: Write

Develop and write a short opinion essay. Be sure to . . .

1. introduce your topic,

2. state your opinion,

3. support your opinion with reasons based on text evidence,

4. use linking words and phrases that connect your opinion and reasons,

5. add a concluding sentence.

Name_____ Date_____

Passage 5: Realistic Fiction
A Coat of Paint

by Anonymous

1   "I want the boat smartened up a bit, Jack. Will you lend a hand this afternoon? Will you help me to give her a fresh coat of paint?"

2   "What is the use of wasting paint over an old thing like that, Grandfather? You only use her for taking out the lobster-pots. I wish we had a good boat. We could hire out to visitors."

3   "'If wishes were horses, beggars would ride,'" the old man said. "Or perhaps they would sail. But I don't have enough money put by for a new boat."

4   "And there is little chance of making any," Jack grumbled.

5   "Well, we must just make the best of what we have got. Even if the *Mary Jane* has seen her best days, she can still be kept spick and span as well as seaworthy."

6   "There would be some sense in keeping a smart little craft which looked nice," Jack argued. "But this old tub is only fit for firewood."

7   "Now, look here, sonny. Suppose I were to say, 'It is no use for an old fellow like me to try to look respectable. I will be done with brush and comb, soap and water, and wear rags. I will leave it for the young folks to be smart and tidy'?"

8   "Oh, you wouldn't do that!" Jack said, looking at his jolly ruddy face and white hair. "Granny would never allow that."

continued

Name_____ Date_____

9   "Right. And I am not going to allow my old *Mary Jane* to be untidy either. But I will manage the job myself if old folks and old boats are not worth your troubling about."

10   Now this made Jack ashamed of his reluctance to help. In the afternoon he came and worked with a will. Finally, the old boat in her new dress looked as if she had grown young again.

11   The fresh paint had such a smart appearance that a little girl passing down to the beach stopped and gazed at it with admiration.

12   "Look, Daddy," she called to her father. "Isn't it a dear little boat? Could we have it to go for a row?"

13   "It certainly looks broad and safe enough for a small girl who finds it difficult to keep still," was his answer. The result was an arrangement to hire the boat at intervals for the rest of the summer season.

14   When the *Mary Jane* was laid up for the winter, Jack and his grandfather counted their earnings. They found that enough had been gained to make up the sum wanted for a new boat. They decided they didn't need one.

15   "That coat of paint was worth something after all," the grandfather said.

Name_____ Date_____

Close Reading 1: Read for Main Ideas and Details

"A Coat of Paint" is mostly about a young boy and his grandfather who give new life to an old boat. Read the realistic fiction and underline key elements of the story. Then complete the graphic organizer using details from the realistic fiction. You can add to the graphic organizer if necessary.

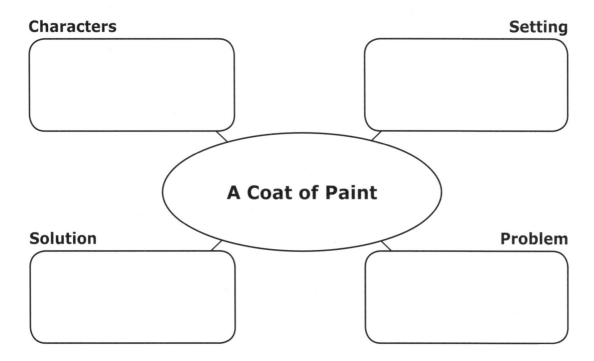

Characters

Setting

A Coat of Paint

Solution

Problem

Collaborative Conversations

Discuss your answers with a partner. When you are the speaker, state your ideas and explain why you think they are key elements of the story. When you are the listener, ask questions to clarify what the speaker says.

Sentence Frames

Speaker: The main characters are . . .

The main problem in the story is . . .

Listener: What details does the author use to describe that?

What can you tell from that detail?

Name_____ Date_____

Close Reading 2: Build Vocabulary

Reread the text. Locate each word or phrase, and identify context clues to determine its meaning. Underline the context clues as you read. Share your definitions or meanings with your partner and check your definitions using a dictionary.

Word or Phrase	Context Clues	What the Text Says It Means
lend a hand		
fellow		
folks		
earnings		

Think-Share-Write

Collaborate with your partner to generate new sentences showing your understanding of each word or phrase. Choose two of the new sentences and write them in the space below.

_____

_____

_____

_____

_____

Name_____ Date_____

Close Reading 3: Identify Text Structure Examples

Part I: Read and Annotate

In this text, the author mainly uses a sequence text structure to tell about a young boy and his grandfather who give new life to an old boat. Reread the text and underline examples of this text structure. Be sure to underline any signal words or phrases used by the author that reinforce the author's use of the sequence text structure.

Part II: Collaborative Conversations

With a partner, discuss your examples using the following questions.

Discussion Questions	Our Notes
1. What text signal words helped you identify your examples?	
2. Did the author always use signal words? Explain how you were able to identify a relationship that did not include signal words.	
3. How does a sequence text structure help you understand the main idea of this text?	
4. Reread paragraphs 1 and 2. The author uses descriptive words like *fresh coat* and *old thing*, but the text structure is sequence. How do these words help you understand the text?	

Part III: Visualize

Draw a picture of what the author wants you to see in paragraphs 11 and 12. Share your drawing with a partner. How are your drawings similar? How are they different?

Name_____ Date_____

Close Reading 4: Build Deeper Understanding

Collaborative Conversations

Reread the text with a partner and discuss the questions. Use information from the text and your annotations to answer the questions. In your discussion, remember to express your ideas clearly and ask questions to better understand each other.

Close Reading Questions	How would you describe Jack at the beginning of the story? How has he changed by the end?	Why do Grandfather and Jack decide not to buy a new boat?	What is the author's purpose for writing this story?
Text Evidence			
Inference/ Answer			

Name_____ Date_____

Apply Knowledge Through Writing

Part I: Collaborative Conversations

With a partner, read and analyze the prompt. Use the following questions in your discussion.

Writing Prompt

In "A Coat of Paint," the author writes about young boy and his grandfather who give new life to an old boat. Do you agree with their decision not to buy a new boat? Support your opinion with reasons based on text evidence.

Analyze the Prompt	My Thoughts
Is this prompt opinion/argument or narrative?	
What is it asking me to write about?	
What are my ideas about this prompt?	

Part II: Write

Develop and write a short opinion essay. Be sure to . . .

    1. introduce your topic,

    2. state your opinion,

    3. support your opinion with reasons based on text evidence,

    4. use linking words and phrases that connect your opinion and reasons,

    5. add a concluding sentence.

Name_____ Date_____

Passage 6: Poem
The Way to Win
by Anonymous

1 "I wish I could win one!" a lassie was sighing,

2 When sitting quite still in a meadow one day,

3 And thinking of prizes not won without trying—

4 Not won by mere wishing as time slips away.

5 And as she sat wishing she heard a hen clucking;

6 She lifted her eyes and that hen she could see,

7 And soon it was rapidly scratching and chucking—

8 As gay and as busy and glad as could be.

9 She watched how it struggled to upturn a treasure,

10 A thing it was wishing for, something to eat,

11 A worm to be dug for with patience and pleasure!

12 'Twas found, and it gave Henny-Penny a treat!

Name_____ Date_____

13 That worm the hen wished for she could not have eaten

14 Unless she had scratched it right up from the ground;

15 And Mabel had seen that the hen was not beaten—

16 By carefully working the prize had been found.

17 So Mabel thought quietly over the matter,

18 And learnt the good lesson, 'No prize can be won

19 By thinking and wishing, by waiting and chatter!'

20 And soon she jumped up and to work she begun.

_____

_____

_____

_____

_____

_____

_____

_____

_____

_____

_____

_____

_____

_____

_____

_____

Name_____ Date_____

Close Reading 1: Read for Main Ideas and Details

"The Way to Win" describes a lesson a girl learns about winning by carefully watching a hen. Read the poem and underline the words that describe the hen's actions. Think about how these actions teach the girl a lesson about winning. Then complete the graphic organizer.

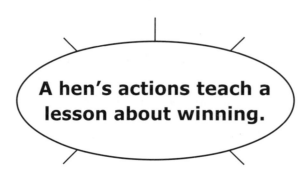

Collaborative Conversations

Discuss your answers with a partner. When you are the speaker, state your ideas and explain why you think the hen's actions teach the girl a lesson about winning. When you are the listener, ask questions to clarify what the speaker says.

Sentence Frames

Speaker: This detail is important because . . .

Based on the information in the text . . .

Listener: Could you tell me more about that detail?

What details does the author use to describe that?

Name_____ Date_____

Close Reading 2: Build Vocabulary

Reread the text. Locate each word or phrase, and identify context clues to determine its meaning. Underline the context clues as you read. Share your definitions or meanings with your partner and check your definitions using a dictionary.

Word or Phrase	Context Clues	What the Text Says It Means
prizes		
slips		
gay		
upturn		

Think-Share-Write

Collaborate with your partner to generate new sentences showing your understanding of each word or phrase. Choose two of the new sentences and write them in the space below.

_____

_____

_____

_____

_____

_____

Name_____ Date_____

Close Reading 3: Identify Text Structure Examples

Part I: Read and Annotate

In this text, the author mainly uses a descriptive text structure to create an image of the hen's actions. Reread the text and underline examples of this text structure. Be sure to underline any signal words or phrases used by the author that reinforce the author's use of the descriptive text structure.

Part II: Collaborative Conversations

With a partner, discuss your examples using the following questions.

Discussion Questions	Our Notes
1. What text signal words helped you identify your examples?	
2. Did the author always use signal words? Explain how you were able to identify a relationship that did not include signal words.	
3. How does a descriptive text structure help you understand the main idea of this text?	
4. Underline the last word in each line. The author uses an ABAB rhyme pattern. How does this pattern affect how the poem sounds?	

Part III: Visualize

Draw a picture of what the author wants you to see while reading the poem. Share your drawing with a partner. How are your drawings similar? How are they different?

Name_____ Date_____

Close Reading 4: Build Deeper Understanding

Collaborative Conversations

Reread the text with a partner and discuss the questions. Use information from the text and your annotations to answer the questions. In your discussion, remember to express your ideas clearly and ask questions to better understand each other.

Close Reading Questions	What is the girl's main problem at the beginning of the poem?	What is the author's point of view about the way to win?	What is the author's purpose for writing this poem?
Text Evidence			
Inference/ Answer			

Name_____ Date_____

Apply Knowledge Through Writing

Part I: Collaborative Conversations

With a partner, read and analyze the prompt. Use the following questions in your discussion.

Writing Prompt

The author of "The Way to Win" uses details to describe a hen's actions. Write a poem that describes another animal's action. Use details to create a picture of the animal and its actions in the reader's mind.

Analyze the Prompt	My Thoughts
Is this prompt narrative or opinion/argument?	
What is it asking me to write about?	
What are my ideas about this prompt?	

Part II: Write

Develop and write a poem. Be sure to . . .

1. describe an animal's actions,

2. use a descriptive text structure,

3. use sensory details, including smell, taste, touch, sound, and sight,

4. use line breaks.

Name_____ Date_____

Passage 7: Historical Fiction
Learning Through My Nose

by Kathleen Bush

1   Early in my life, I learned three important lessons through my nose. The first lesson was that humans rarely eat all of the food that they put on their plates. At the end of a meal, they usually scrape perfectly good food into the trash bin unless a dog like me is there to claim it.

2   I was trying to claim some food when I first met Robert Conroy in 1917. It was a hot summer day at the military training camp in New Haven, Connecticut. I had been making my rounds of the camp tents, sniffing to find out which soldiers had food. I used my eyes to politely tell them that I was willing to eat their leftovers.

3   When I sniffed out Robert, it was more than just his food that caught my nose's attention. It was also his deep kindness. But on that first day, all I knew was that I had made a new friend. That was when I learned my second lesson through my nose. Some humans need my attention more than others. I was reminded of that lesson many times in the months that followed.

4   One night at the end of the summer, the soldiers packed up their supplies. They boarded a ship with me that carried us over the ocean to the war in Europe. At the time, I didn't understand the word *war*. But I could smell the soldiers' fear. I discovered that I could make that smell get weaker when I made the men laugh. So I spent my time performing the soldier salute that Robert had taught me.

continued

Name_____ Date_____

5   When we finally arrived in France, I soon came to understand why the word *war* smelled like fear. For a long while, we lived in muddy trenches that the men had dug deep in the ground. Digging and rolling in the dirt felt natural to me. But I could smell Robert's discomfort. I tried to keep him warm by pressing my body against his.

6   There were often loud explosions that shook the ground and covered us in mud. Sometimes my nose told me that some soldiers in our division were hurt by those explosions. I would sniff them out and bark for help. I was hurt several times myself and taken to a military hospital. I was always relieved to return to Robert in the trenches.

7   The war is finally over. We are safely back in the United States together. I can no longer smell fear on Robert. He takes me to ceremonies where people pin medals on my vest. He takes me to parades where people cheer for me.

8   "Hooray for Stubby the war dog!" they shout.

9   At first, I was confused by this attention. Why were they cheering? But when my nose picked up the happiness at these events, I learned my third lesson. Humans need a hero.

Name_____ Date_____

Close Reading 1: Read for Main Ideas and Details

"Learning Through My Nose" is mostly about a military dog's experience in a war. Read the historical fiction text and underline the key elements of the story. Then complete the graphic organizer using details from the historical fiction text. You can add to the graphic organizer if necessary.

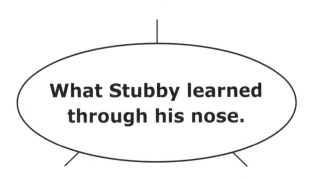

What Stubby learned through his nose.

Collaborative Conversations

Discuss your answers with a partner. When you are the speaker, state your ideas and explain why you think they are key details about Stubby's experience in a war. When you are the listener, ask questions to clarify what the speaker says.

Sentence Frames

Speaker: The most important idea in the story . . .

I know this because . . .

Listener: Why did you choose this detail?

Could you tell me more about this idea?

Name_____ Date_____

Close Reading 2: Build Vocabulary

Reread the text. Locate each word or phrase, and identify context clues to determine its meaning. Underline the context clues as you read. Share your definitions or meanings with your partner and check your definitions using a dictionary.

Word or Phrase	Context Clues	What the Text Says It Means
rarely		
making my rounds		
trenches		
ceremonies		
cheer		
confused		

Think-Share-Write

Collaborate with your partner to generate new sentences showing your understanding of each word or phrase. Choose two of the new sentences and write them in the space below.

_____

_____

_____

_____

Name_____ Date_____

Close Reading 3: Identify Text Structure Examples

Part I: Read and Annotate

In this text, the author mainly uses a sequence text structure to tell about Stubby's experience in war. Reread the text and underline examples of this text structure. Be sure to underline any signal words or phrases used by the author that reinforce the author's use of the sequence text structure.

Part II: Collaborative Conversations

With a partner, discuss your examples using the following questions.

Discussion Questions	Our Notes
1. What text signal words helped you identify your examples?	
2. Did the author always use signal words? Explain how you were able to identify a relationship that did not include signal words.	
3. How does a sequence text structure help you understand the main idea of this text?	
4. Reread paragraph 6. The author uses descriptive words like *loud*, *shook*, and *covered us*, but the text structure is sequence. How do these words help you understand the text?	

Part III: Visualize

Draw a picture of what the author wants you to see in paragraphs 7 and 8. Share your drawing with a partner. How are your drawings similar? How are they different?

Name_____ Date_____

Close Reading 4: Build Deeper Understanding

Collaborative Conversations

Reread the text with a partner and discuss the questions. Use information from the text and your annotations to answer the questions. In your discussion, remember to express your ideas clearly and ask questions to better understand each other.

Close Reading Questions	What do the three lessons Stubby learns through his nose tell us about Stubby's point of view about his role in the lives of humans?	How does Stubby help soldiers during war?	What is the author's purpose for writing this text?
Text Evidence			
Inference/ Answer			

Name_____ Date_____

Apply Knowledge Through Writing

Part I: Collaborative Conversations

With a partner, read and analyze the prompt. Use the following questions in your discussion.

Writing Prompt

In "Learning Through My Nose," the author writes about a dog's experiences in war. The text is written from the dog's own point of view. Write a short story that tells what Stubby did from his master Robert's point of view. Support your ideas with information from the text.

Analyze the Prompt	My Thoughts
Is this prompt informative/ explanatory or narrative?	
What is it asking me to write about?	
What are my ideas about this prompt?	

Part II: Write

Develop and write a short narrative. Be sure to . . .

1. begin the narrative using time and place,

2. introduce your characters or the narrator of the story,

3. develop the characters through actions and events,

4. use signal words showing time,

5. add an ending.

Name_____ Date_____

Passage 8: Science Article
Feelin' Frazzled
by Centers for Disease Control and Prevention

1 Forgetting your homework or missing your ride home can really stress you out. Are you looking for a safety net for those days that seem to get worse by the second? Could you really use some advice on how to de-stress? Knowing how to deal can be half the battle. Check out these tips to keep you cool and calm.

Put Your Body in Motion

2 Whether you like games of basketball or you like walks with family, it's important to get moving! Physical activity is one of the most important ways to keep stress away by clearing your head. Physical activity also increases endorphin levels. Endorphins are the natural "feel-good" chemicals in the body that leave you with a happy feeling.

Fuel Up

3 Start your day off with a full tank. Eating breakfast will give you the energy you need to tackle the day. Eating regular meals and taking time to enjoy them will make you feel better, too. Make sure to fuel up with fruits and vegetables. Also, eat proteins, such as peanut butter and grains. These will give you the power you need to make it through those hectic days.

Take Time to Chill

4 Pick a comfy spot to sit and read. Listen to your favorite music. Work on a relaxing project—put a puzzle together or make jewelry. Stress can sometimes make you feel like a tight rubber band—stretched to the limit! If this happens, take

Name_____ Date_____

a few deep breaths to help yourself unwind. If you're in the middle of an impossible homework problem, take a break! Finding time to relax can make all the difference.

Catch Some Zzzzz . . .

5 Fatigue is a best friend to stress. When you don't get enough sleep, it's hard to do your best. You may feel tired or cranky. You may even have trouble thinking clearly. When you're overtired, a problem may seem much bigger than it actually is. You may have a hard time doing a school assignment that usually seems easy. You may even have an argument with your friends over something really small.

6   Sleep is a big deal! Getting the right amount of sleep is especially important for kids your age. Your body and mind are changing and developing. It requires more sleep to re-charge for the next day. So don't resist—hit the hay!

7   Most importantly, don't sweat the small stuff! Try to pick a few really important things and let the rest slide. Getting worked up over every little thing will only increase your stress. So toughen up and don't let stressful situations get to you! Remember, you're not alone. Everyone has stresses in their lives. It's up to you to choose how to deal with them.

Passage 8 • Science Article

Name_____ Date_____

Close Reading 1: Read for Details and Main Ideas

"Feelin' Frazzled" is mostly about ways to deal with stress. Read the science article and underline the key details that tell how to deal with stress. Then complete the graphic organizer using details from the science article. You can add to the graphic organizer if necessary.

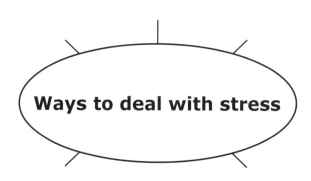

Ways to deal with stress

Collaborative Conversations

Discuss your answers with a partner. When you are the speaker, state your ideas and explain why you think they explain ways to deal with stress. When you are the listener, ask questions to clarify what the speaker says.

Sentence Frames

Speaker: The most important idea in the text . . .

The author's main point is . . .

Listener: Could you tell me more about this idea?

What details does the author use to describe that?

Name_____ Date_____

Close Reading 2: Build Vocabulary

Reread the text. Locate each word or phrase, and identify context clues to determine its meaning. Underline the context clues as you read. Share your definitions or meanings with your partner and check your definitions using a dictionary.

Word or Phrase	Context Clues	What the Text Says It Means
stress		
endorphins		
proteins		
fatigue		

Think-Share-Write

Collaborate with your partner to generate new sentences showing your understanding of each word or phrase. Choose two of the new sentences and write them in the space below.

_____

_____

_____

_____

Name_____ Date_____

Close Reading 3: Identify Text Structure Examples

Part I: Read and Annotate

In this text, the author mainly uses a problem/solution text structure to tell about ways to deal with stress. Reread the text and underline examples of this text structure. Be sure to underline any signal words or phrases used by the author that reinforce the author's use of the problem/solution text structure.

Part II: Collaborative Conversations

With a partner, discuss your examples using the following questions.

Discussion Questions	Our Notes
1. What signal words or phrases helped you identify your examples?	
2. Did the author always use signal words? Explain how you were able to identify a relationship that did not include signal words.	
3. How does a problem/solution text structure help you understand the main idea of this text?	
4. Reread paragraph 7. The author uses the signal words *most importantly*, *so*, and *remember*. How do these words help you understand the text?	

Part III: Visualize

Draw a picture of what the author wants you to see in paragraph 4. Share your drawing with a partner. How are your drawings similar? How are they different?

Name_____ Date_____

Close Reading 4: Build Deeper Understanding

Collaborative Conversations

Reread the text with a partner and discuss the questions. Use information from the text and your annotations to answer the questions. In your discussion, remember to express your ideas clearly and ask questions to better understand each other.

Close Reading Questions	What is the author's purpose for writing this article?	What does the author mean by "don't sweat the small stuff"? What might the author consider "small stuff"? Explain your answer.	What is the author's point of view about stress?
Text Evidence			
Inference/ Answer			

Name_____ Date_____

Apply Knowledge Through Writing

Part I: Collaborative Conversations

With a partner, read and analyze the prompt. Use the following questions in your discussion.

Writing Prompt

In "Feelin' Frazzled," the author tells about ways to deal with stress. Write a short essay that tells about a time you dealt with stress. What was the cause of the stress? How did you deal with it? Connect your ideas to the ideas presented in the text.

Analyze the Prompt	My Thoughts
Is this prompt opinion/argument or informative/explanatory?	
What is it asking me to write about?	
What are my ideas about this prompt?	

Part II: Write

Develop and write a short informative essay. Be sure to . . .

    1. state your topic,

    2. use details and text evidence to develop the topic,

    3. use linking words and phrases,

    4. add a concluding sentence.

Name_____ Date_____

Passage 9: Biography
Cesar Chavez

from America's Library

1   Cesar Chavez was one of six children. His parents owned a ranch and a small grocery store. During the Great Depression they lost everything. In order to survive, Cesar Chavez and his family became migrant farm workers. Migrants are people who move from place to place in order to find work. It was hard, and they did not live in the same place for long. The Chavez family would pick lettuce in the winter, cherries in the spring, grapes in the summer, and cotton in the fall.

2   Working conditions for migrant workers were harsh and unsafe. Their wages were low and it was difficult to support a family. Cesar's family often did not have access to basic needs like clean water or toilets. Because a large number of migrant workers were Mexican American, they also often faced prejudice. Cesar Chavez attended about thirty schools as his family moved from place to place to find work. After the eighth grade, Cesar had to quit school to support his parents.

3   Cesar's life growing up had a big impact on what he did the rest of his life. He married a woman who also was from a family of migrant farm workers. The couple had eight children. Chavez had little education and training. He was forced to return to farm work. As before, life in the fields was harsh. Chavez decided he had to do something about it. He united farm workers into a labor union.

continued

Name_____ Date_____

4   Cesar's union refused to work until there were better conditions. This strike lasted for five years. But Cesar's leadership focused national attention on the terrible working conditions. Cesar used peaceful methods and got public support for the union. He and the union won better contracts for higher wages and better treatment of workers.

Name_____ Date_____

Close Reading 1: Read for Main Ideas and Details

"Cesar Chavez" is mostly about a migrant farm worker who helped improve working conditions for farm workers. Read the biography and underline the key details that support the main idea. Then complete the graphic organizer using details from the biography. You can add to the graphic organizer if necessary.

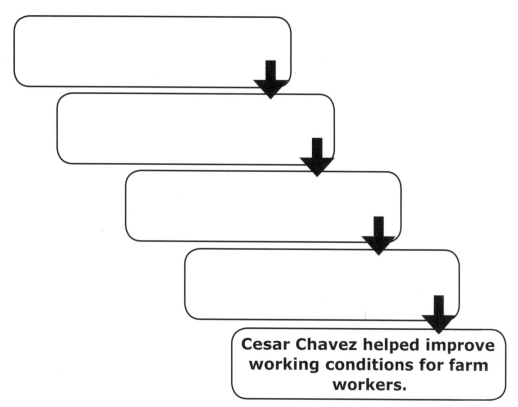

Cesar Chavez helped improve working conditions for farm workers.

Collaborative Conversations

Discuss your answers with a partner. When you are the speaker, state your ideas and explain why you think they are important details about how Cesar Chavez helped improve working conditions for farm workers. When you are the listener, ask questions to clarify what the speaker says.

Sentence Frames

Speaker: A key idea that supports the main idea is . . .

I know this because . . .

Listener: Tell me why you chose this detail.

Could you tell me more about this idea?

Name_____ Date_____

Close Reading 2: Build Vocabulary

Reread the text. Locate each word or phrase, and identify context clues to determine its meaning. Underline the context clues as you read. Share your definitions or meanings with your partner and check your definitions using a dictionary.

Word or Phrase	Context Clues	What the Text Says It Means
migrant		
conditions		
wages		
labor union		
strike		

Think-Share-Write

Collaborate with your partner to generate new sentences showing your understanding of each word or phrase. Choose two of the new sentences and write them in the space below.

_____

_____

_____

_____

Name_____ Date_____

Close Reading 3: Identify Text Structure Examples

Part I: Read and Annotate

In this text, the author mainly uses a sequence text structure to tell about the life of Cesar Chavez. Reread the text and underline examples of this text structure. Be sure to underline any signal words or phrases used by the author that reinforce the author's use of the sequence text structure.

Part II: Collaborative Conversations

With a partner, discuss your examples using the following questions.

Discussion Questions	Our Notes
1. What text signal words or phrases helped you identify your examples?	
2. Did the author always use signal words? Explain how you were able to identify a relationship that did not include signal words.	
3. How does a sequence text structure help you understand the main idea of this text?	
4. Reread paragraph 2. The author uses descriptive words like *harsh*, *unsafe*, and *difficult* but the text structure is sequence. How do these words help you understand the text?	

Part III: Visualize

Draw a picture of what the author wants you to see in paragraphs 1 and 2. Share your drawing with a partner. How are your drawings similar? How are they different?

Passage 9 • Biography

Name_____ Date_____

Close Reading 4: Build Deeper Understanding

Collaborative Conversations

Reread the text with a partner and discuss the questions. Use information from the text and your annotations to answer the questions. In your discussion, remember to express your ideas clearly and ask questions to better understand each other.

Close Reading Questions	What is the author's point of view about Cesar Chavez? What words or phrases help you identify that point of view?	The author does not give details about the strike. What does this tell you about the author's purpose?	How would this text be different if it were written from a farm owner's point of view?
Text Evidence			
Inference/ Answer			

Name_____ Date_____

Apply Knowledge Through Writing

Part I: Collaborative Conversations

With a partner, read and analyze the prompt. Use the following questions in your discussion.

Writing Prompt

In "Cesar Chavez," the author tells about the working conditions for migrant farm workers. Write a narrative that describes how Chavez united workers to improve their working conditions. Support your writing with evidence from the text.

Analyze the Prompt	My Thoughts
Is this prompt narrative or opinion/argument?	
What is it asking me to write about?	
What are my ideas about this prompt?	

Part II: Write

Develop and write a short narrative. Be sure to . . .

1. begin the narrative using time and place,

2. introduce your characters or the narrator of the story,

3. develop the characters through actions and events,

4. use signal words showing time,

5. add an ending.

Name_____ Date_____

Passage 10: Speech
President Obama's Back-to-School Remarks

1   I know that sometimes you get the sense from TV that you can be rich and successful without any hard work. That your ticket to success is through rapping or basketball or being a reality TV star. The chances are, you're not going to be any of those things.

2   The truth is, being successful is hard. You won't love every subject you study. You won't click with every teacher. Not every homework assignment will seem completely relevant to your life right this minute. And you won't necessarily succeed at everything the first time you try.

3   That's okay. Some of the most successful people in the world are the ones who've had the most failures. J.K. Rowling's first Harry Potter book was rejected twelve times before it was finally published. Michael Jordan was cut from his high school basketball team, and he lost hundreds of games and missed thousands of shots during his career. But he once said, "I have failed over and over and over again in my life. And that is why I succeed."

Name_____ Date_____

4   No one's born being good at things; you become good at things through hard work. You're not a varsity athlete the first time you play a new sport. You don't hit every note the first time you sing a song. You've got to practice. It's the same with your schoolwork. You might have to do a math problem a few times before you get it right, or read something a few times before you understand it, or do a few drafts of a paper before it's good enough to hand in.

5   The story of America isn't about people who quit when things got tough. It's about people who kept going, who tried harder, who loved their country too much to do anything less than their best.

6   So today I want to ask you, what's your contribution going to be? What problems are you going to solve? What discoveries will you make? What will a president who comes here in twenty or fifty or one hundred years say about what all of you did for this country?

Passage 10 • Speech

Name_____ Date_____

Close Reading 1: Read for Main Ideas and Details

"President Obama's Back-to-School Remarks" is mostly about how success takes hard work. Read the speech and underline the key details that support the main idea. Then complete the graphic organizer using details from the speech. You can add to the graphic organizer if necessary.

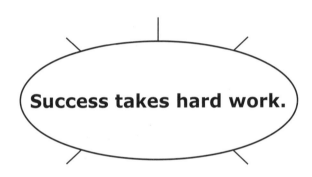

Collaborative Conversations

Discuss your answers with a partner. When you are the speaker, state your ideas and explain why you think they support the idea that success takes hard work. When you are the listener, ask questions to clarify what the speaker says.

Sentence Frames

Speaker: The speaker's main point is . . .

Based on the information in the speech . . .

Listener: What evidence in the speech leads you to say that?

What details does the speaker use to describe that?

Name_____ Date_____

Close Reading 2: Build Vocabulary

Reread the text. Locate each word or phrase, and identify context clues to determine its meaning. Underline the context clues as you read. Share your definitions or meanings with your partner and check your definitions using a dictionary.

Word or Phrase	Context Clues	What the Text Says It Means
relevant		
drafts		
click		
published		
contribution		

Think-Share-Write

Collaborate with your partner to generate new sentences showing your understanding of each word or phrase. Choose two of the new sentences and write them in the space below.

_____

_____

_____

Name_____ Date_____

Close Reading 3: Identify Text Structure Examples

Part I: Read and Annotate

In this text, the author mainly uses a descriptive text structure to explain that success takes hard work. Reread the text and underline examples of this text structure. Be sure to underline any signal words or phrases used by the author that reinforce the author's use of the descriptive text structure.

Part II: Collaborative Conversations

With a partner, discuss your examples using the following questions.

Discussion Questions	Our Notes
1. What text signal words helped you identify your examples?	
2. Did the author always use signal words? Explain how you were able to identify a relationship that did not include signal words.	
3. How does a descriptive text structure help you understand the main idea of this text?	
4. Reread paragraph 6. The author uses questions like "What problems are you going to solve?" and "What discoveries will you make?" but the text structure is descriptive. How do these questions help you understand the text?	

Part III: Visualize

Draw a picture of what the author wants you to see in paragraph 4. Share your drawing with a partner. How are your drawings similar? How are they different?

Name_____ Date_____

Close Reading 4: Build Deeper Understanding

Collaborative Conversations

Reread the text with a partner and discuss the questions. Use information from the text and your annotations to answer the questions. In your discussion, remember to express your ideas clearly and ask questions to better understand each other.

Close Reading Questions	What can you tell about the speaker from his description of school in paragraph 2?	What is the speaker's purpose?	What is the speaker's point of view about success and failure?
Text Evidence			
Inference/ Answer			

Name_____ Date_____

Apply Knowledge Through Writing

Part I: Collaborative Conversations

With a partner, read and analyze the prompt. Use the following questions in your discussion.

Writing Prompt

In "President Obama's Back-to-School Remarks," the speaker explains that failure is an important part of success. Do you agree or disagree with this message? Write a short essay that states your opinion. Support your opinion with reasons based on text evidence.

Analyze the Prompt	My Thoughts
Is this prompt narrative or opinion/argument?	
What is it asking me to write about?	
What are my ideas about this prompt?	

Part II: Write

Develop and write a short opinion essay. Be sure to . . .

1. introduce your topic,

2. state your opinion,

3. support your opinion with reasons based on text evidence,

4. use linking words and phrases that connect your opinion and reasons,

5. add a concluding sentence.

Name_____ Date_____

Passage 11: How-To Article
How to Bake Bread at Home

by Kristin Marciniak

1   The best bread doesn't come from the grocery store. It comes straight from your oven at home! All you need is flour, water, yeast, corn meal, and a big pot with a lid.

2   This is a great recipe for first-time bread bakers. It takes longer to finish than other bread recipes, but it takes only ten minutes of work. That's because of the way you handle, or in this case, don't handle, the dough.

3   Most bread dough requires kneading. That's when you use your hands to push and fold the dough over and over again. When you knead dough, you're helping create gluten. Gluten is a kind of protein. The more you knead, the stronger the gluten becomes. Strong strands of gluten help the bread dough rise, or grow larger. A good rise improves the taste and feel of the bread.

4   But dough doesn't have to be kneaded for gluten to form. It forms on its own if the dough is left alone long enough. It happens slowly, which is why a lot of people knead their dough instead. But if you're not in a hurry, this recipe is for you.

5   You will need:

6   • 3 cups flour

7   • 1 1/2 cups water

8   • 1/2 teaspoon instant yeast

9   • corn meal

continued

Name_____ Date_____

10   1. In a large bowl, mix the flour and yeast. Add water and stir. The dough will be shaggy and sticky. Cover the bowl with plastic wrap. Let it sit on the counter for 12–18 hours.

11   2. The dough is ready when it is dotted with bubbles. Spread a handful of flour onto a clean countertop or table. Rub flour on your hands, too. Then dump the dough onto the floured counter. Add a little more flour on top of the dough. Fold the dough in half, then fold in half again. Gently lay a piece of plastic wrap on top. Let the dough rest for at least 15 minutes.

12   3. Spread a handful of corn meal or flour onto a clean kitchen towel. Quickly shape the dough into a ball, using flour as needed to keep it from sticking to your hands. Place dough onto towel. Dust with more cornmeal or flour. Cover with another towel. Let dough rest for two hours. Dough will double in size during this time.

13   4. Put a large oven-safe pot, covered with a lid, onto the lowest rack of the oven. Heat the oven to 450°F 30 minutes before baking. Put on oven mitts and carefully remove the hot pot from the oven. Place the pot on a heat-safe surface, like the top of the stove. Dump dough into the pot. Put the oven mitts back on and shake the pot a few times so dough spreads evenly.

14   5. Put the lid on the pot and bake for 30 minutes. Remove the lid and bake for another 15–30 minutes, or until the bread's crust is a deep brown. Cool completely before cutting.

Name_____ Date_____

Close Reading 1: Read for Main Ideas and Details

"How to Bake Bread at Home" is mostly about baking bread with very little work. Read the how-to article and underline the key details that support the main idea. Then complete the graphic organizer using details from the how-to article. You can add to the graphic organizer if necessary.

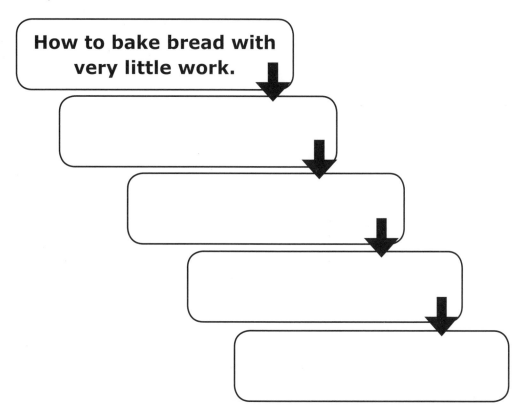

How to bake bread with very little work.

Collaborative Conversations

Discuss your answers with a partner. When you are the speaker, state your ideas and explain why you think they are key steps to baking bread with very little work. When you are the listener, ask questions to clarify what the speaker says.

Sentence Frames

Speaker: A key step is . . .

I chose this step because . . .

Listener: Tell me why you chose this step.

Could you tell me more about this idea?

Name_____ Date_____

Close Reading 2: Build Vocabulary

Reread the text. Locate each word or phrase, and identify context clues to determine its meaning. Underline the context clues as you read. Share your definitions or meanings with your partner and check your definitions using a dictionary.

Word or Phrase	Context Clues	What the Text Says It Means
recipe		
kneading		
improves		
spread		
heat		

Think-Share-Write

Collaborate with your partner to generate new sentences showing your understanding of each word or phrase. Choose two of the new sentences and write them in the space below.

_____

_____

_____

_____

Name_____ Date_____

Close Reading 3: Identify Text Structure Examples

Part I: Read and Annotate

In this text, the author mainly uses a sequence text structure to tell readers how to bake bread. Reread the text and underline examples of this text structure. Be sure to underline any signal words or phrases used by the author that reinforce the author's use of the sequence text structure.

Part II: Collaborative Conversations

With a partner, discuss your examples using the following questions.

Discussion Questions	Our Notes
1. What text signal words helped you identify your examples?	
2. Did the author always use signal words? Explain how you were able to identify a relationship that did not include signal words.	
3. How does a sequence text structure help you understand the main idea of this text?	
4. Reread paragraph 2. The author uses the cause/effect word *because*, but the text structure is sequence. How does this word help you understand the text?	

Part III: Visualize

Draw a picture of what the author wants you to see in step 2. Share your drawing with a partner. How are your drawings similar? How are they different?

Name_____ Date_____

Close Reading 4: Build Deeper Understanding

Collaborative Conversations

Reread the text with a partner and discuss the questions. Use information from the text and your annotations to answer the questions. In your discussion, remember to express your ideas clearly and ask questions to better understand each other.

Close Reading Questions	What is the author's purpose for writing this recipe?	What is the author's point of view about homemade bread?	Why is this recipe good for first-time bread bakers?
Text Evidence			
Inference/ Answer			

Name_____ Date_____

Apply Knowledge Through Writing

Part I: Collaborative Conversations

With a partner, read and analyze the prompt. Use the following questions in your discussion.

Writing Prompt

In "How to Bake Bread at Home," the author writes about baking bread with very little work. Imagine that you followed this recipe at home. Write a short story about your experience. Support your ideas with information from the text.

Analyze the Prompt	My Thoughts
Is this prompt narrative or informative/explanatory?	
What is it asking me to write about?	
What are my ideas about this prompt?	

Part II: Write

Develop and write a short narrative. Be sure to . . .

1. begin the narrative using time and place,

2. introduce your characters or the narrator of the story,

3. develop the characters through actions and events,

4. use signal words showing time,

5. add an ending.

Name_____ Date_____

Passage 12: Science Article
Ecosystems

by Michelle Olmsted

1   An ecosystem includes the plants and animals that live in an area. All living things in an ecosystem depend on one another to survive. They also depend on their environment, or surroundings. We will look at three types of ecosystems: deserts, grasslands, and rain forests.

Deserts

2   The world's deserts make up one-quarter of Earth's land. Deserts are dry areas that get very little rain per year. The desert is very hot during the day, and cold at night.

3   The plants and animals that live in the desert have adapted, or adjusted, to living in this hot and dry area. A desert plant, such as a cactus, needs very little water to survive.

4   Coyotes, rattlesnakes, and jackrabbits are some of the animals that live in deserts. Many desert animals are light in color. Light colors take in less heat. And their light color helps them hide from predators, or hunters. Most desert animals sleep during the day and hunt at night when it is cooler.

Grasslands

5   Deserts can be hilly or flat, but grasslands are stretches of flat land. They are covered in grasses and wildflowers. This ecosystem is often located between deserts and forests. Grasslands get more rain than deserts. But there is not enough rain to grow tall trees. So grasslands are often used to grow crops, like wheat and corn.

Name_____ Date_____

6   The large expanses of flat land offer few hiding places for animals. So many grassland animals have colorations that allow them to blend in with their surroundings. And many animals live within herds for protection. Wolves, turkeys, snakes, and rabbits live in grasslands.

Rain Forests

7   Rain forests are Earth's oldest living ecosystems. They are named for the high amount of rainfall they receive per year and the tall trees that fill the land.

8   Rain forests cover a very small portion of Earth's surface. However, they contain more than half of the world's plant and animal species—the most of any ecosystem. That is because rain forests provide a rich supply of water and food.

9   Many rain forest animals use the tall trees as shelter and a source of food. There are many small and colorful animals in the rain forest. Some of them, like monkeys, birds, and frogs, never even touch the ground!

Passage 12 • Science Article

Name_____ Date_____

Close Reading 1: Read for Main Ideas and Details

"Ecosystems" is mostly about three types of ecosystems: deserts, grasslands, and rain forests. Read the science article and underline the key details that support the main idea. Then complete the graphic organizer using details from the science article. You can add to the graphic organizer if necessary.

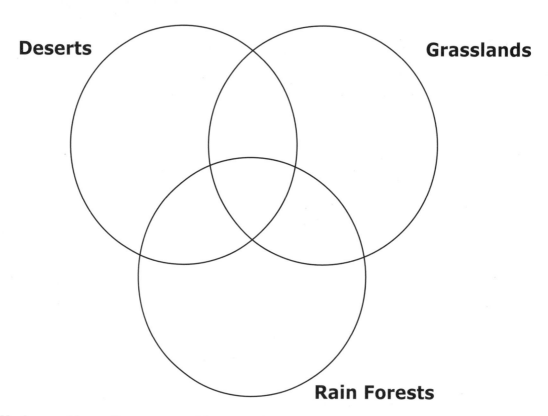

Deserts   **Grasslands**

Rain Forests

Collaborative Conversations

Discuss your answers with a partner. When you are the speaker, state your ideas and explain why you think they are key details about the three different types of ecosystems. When you are the listener, ask questions to clarify what the speaker says.

Sentence Frames

Speaker: Based on the information in the text . . .

I know this because . . .

Listener: Why did you choose this detail?

Could you tell me more about this idea?

Conquer Close Reading Grade 3 • ©2015 Newmark Learning, LLC

Name_____ Date_____

Close Reading 2: Build Vocabulary

Reread the text. Locate each word or phrase, and identify context clues to determine its meaning. Underline the context clues as you read. Share your definitions or meanings with your partner and check your definitions using a dictionary.

Word or Phrase	Context Clues	What the Text Says It Means
depend		
environment		
adapted		
predators		

Think-Share-Write

Collaborate with your partner to generate new sentences showing your understanding of each word or phrase. Choose two of the new sentences and write them in the space below.

_____

_____

_____

_____

_____

Name_____ Date_____

Close Reading 3: Identify Text Structure Examples

Part I: Read and Annotate

In this text, the author mainly uses a compare/contrast text structure to tell about deserts, grasslands, and rain forests. Reread the text and underline examples of this text structure. Be sure to underline any signal words or phrases used by the author that reinforce the author's use of the compare/contrast text structure.

Part II: Collaborative Conversations

With a partner, discuss your examples using the following questions.

Discussion Questions	Our Notes
1. What text signal words helped you identify your examples?	
2. Did the author always use signal words? Explain how you were able to identify a relationship that did not include signal words.	
3. How does a compare/contrast text structure help you understand the main idea of this text?	
4. Reread paragraphs 5 and 6. The author uses the cause/effect word *so*, but the text structure is compare/contrast. How does this signal word help you understand the text?	

Part III: Visualize

Draw a picture of what the author wants you to see in paragraph 9. Share your drawing with a partner. How are your drawings similar? How are they different?

Name_____ Date_____

Close Reading 4: Build Deeper Understanding

Collaborative Conversations

Reread the text with a partner and discuss the questions. Use information from the text and your annotations to answer the questions. In your discussion, remember to express your ideas clearly and ask questions to better understand each other.

Close Reading Questions	How do both desert and grassland animals hide from predators?	What makes rain forests different from any other ecosystem on the planet?	What is the author's purpose for writing this article?
Text Evidence			
Inference/ Answer			

Name_____ Date_____

Apply Knowledge Through Writing

Part I: Collaborative Conversations

With a partner, read and analyze the prompt. Use the following questions in your discussion.

Writing Prompt

In "Ecosystems," the author writes about three types of ecosystems: deserts, grasslands, and rain forests. Write a short story about an animal or group of animals that live in one of these ecosystems. Support your ideas with information from the text.

Analyze the Prompt	My Thoughts
Is this prompt opinion/argument or narrative?	
What is it asking me to write about?	
What are my ideas about this prompt?	

Part II: Write

Develop and write a short narrative. Be sure to . . .

1. begin the narrative using time and place,

2. introduce your characters or the narrator of the story,

3. develop the characters through actions and events,

4. use signal words showing time,

5. add an ending.

Name_____ Date_____

Passage 13: Social Studies Article
Artistic Olympians

by Kathleen Bush

1   What do you think of when you read the words *Olympic Games*? You might think of the competitions that take place every four years. You might think of summer sports like cycling or volleyball. You might think of winter sports like skating or snowboarding. Or you might think of hundreds of athletes from around the world. What you might not think of is art. Yet art was part of the early modern Olympic Games.

The Early Olympic Games

2   From 1912 until 1952, Olympians could compete in art as well as in sports events. There were competitions in architecture, music, painting, sculpture, and literature. The rule was that the art had to be inspired by sport. In this way, art and sports were closely connected. In fact, some of the Olympians who competed in sports also competed in arts. At the 1912 Olympic Games, for example, American Walter Winans won a gold medal for the sport of sharpshooting. He also won a gold medal for his sculpture *An American Trotter*.

continued →

Name_____ Date_____

The Arts Olympiad

3 This connection of art and sports has not been forgotten. In recent years, the International Child Art Foundation has organized the Arts Olympiad every four years. The Arts Olympiad is an art competition. However, it focuses on the theme of sports. Children between the ages of eight and twelve in schools all over the world create artwork about sports. Artwork from each school is then sent to a panel of judges. The winners are invited to the World Children's Festival in Washington, D.C.

4 The goal of the events is to show that everyone can be both an artist and an athlete. Everyone can have both a creative mind and a healthy body. Nelson Mandela once said that art and sports "are instruments for peace, even more powerful than governments." Maybe the artistic Olympians of these events will prove that Mandela's words are true.

Name_____ Date_____

Close Reading 1: Read for Main Ideas and Details

"Artistic Olympians" is mostly about the connection between art and sports. Read the social studies article and underline the key details that support the main idea. Then complete the graphic organizer using details from the social studies article. You can add to the graphic organizer if necessary.

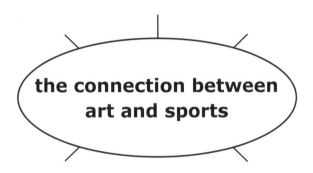

the connection between
art and sports

Collaborative Conversations

Discuss your answers with a partner. When you are the speaker, state your ideas and explain why you think they support the idea that art and sports are connected. When you are the listener, ask questions to clarify what the speaker says.

Sentence Frames

A key idea that supports the main idea is . . .

The author's main point is . . .

Listener: What evidence in the text leads you to say that?

What details does the author use to describe that?

Name_____ Date_____

Close Reading 2: Build Vocabulary

Reread the text. Locate each word or phrase, and identify context clues to determine its meaning. Underline the context clues as you read. Share your definitions or meanings with your partner and check your definitions using a dictionary.

Word or Phrase	Context Clues	What the Text Says It Means
Olympic Games		
Olympians		
connected		
goal		

Think-Share-Write

Collaborate with your partner to generate new sentences showing your understanding of each word or phrase. Choose two of the new sentences and write them in the space below.

_____

_____

_____

_____

Name_____ Date_____

Close Reading 3: Identify Text Structure Examples

Part I: Read and Annotate

In this text, the author mainly uses a descriptive text structure to describe the connection between art and sports. Reread the text and underline examples of this text structure. Be sure to underline any signal words or phrases used by the author that reinforce the author's use of the descriptive text structure.

Part II: Collaborative Conversations

With a partner, discuss your examples using the following questions.

Discussion Questions	Our Notes
1. What text signal words helped you identify your examples?	
2. Does the author always use signal words? Explain how you were able to identify a relationship that did not include signal words.	
3. How does a descriptive text structure help you understand the main idea of this text?	
4. Reread paragraphs 2 and 3. The author uses sequence phrases like "From 1912 until 1952" and "In recent years," but the text structure is descriptive. How do these words help you understand the text?	

Part III: Visualize

Draw a picture of what the author wants you to see in paragraph 3. Share your drawing with a partner. How are your drawings similar? How are they different?

Name_____ Date_____

Close Reading 4: Build Deeper Understanding

Collaborative Conversations

Reread the text with a partner and discuss the questions. Use information from the text and your annotations to answer the questions. In your discussion, remember to express your ideas clearly and ask questions to better understand each other.

Close Reading Questions	What was the purpose of including art at the Olympic Games?	How are art and sports "instruments of peace"?	What is the author's purpose for writing this article?
Text Evidence			
Inference/ Answer			

Name_____ Date_____

Apply Knowledge Through Writing

Part I: Collaborative Conversations

With a partner, read and analyze the prompt. Use the following questions in your discussion.

Writing Prompt

In "Artistic Olympians," the author writes about the connection between art and sports. Write a short informative essay that describes a specific connection between art and a sporting event. Support your ideas with information from the text.

Analyze the Prompt	My Thoughts
Is this prompt informative/ explanatory or opinion/argument?	
What is it asking me to write about?	
What are my ideas about this prompt?	

Part II: Write

Develop and write a short informative essay. Be sure to . . .

1. state your topic,

2. use details and text evidence to develop the topic,

3. use linking words and phrases,

4. add a concluding sentence.

Name_____ Date_____

Passage 14: Opinion/Argument Piece
Down with Homework!

by Sarah Boyle

1   You've just spent seven hours sitting at a desk working on your reading, writing, and arithmetic. Now you're at home. You just want to relax with a glass of milk and a crispy apple. But no! Your dad sits you down at the kitchen table to work on that big pile of homework you brought home.

2   Elementary school teachers assign their students too much homework. According to the Brookings Institution's Brown Center on Education Policy, the amount of homework third graders take home has increased since 1984. And that homework is stressing out both kids and their parents.

3   Kids in elementary school have less time to play than they did three decades ago. They also have less time to bond with their families. There's no time for a game of catch with Mom. Instead, Mom and her daughter pull out their hair as they try to figure out a tricky math worksheet. Family board game night gets put off again. Instead, the son sits at his desk, alone, working on a lengthy research project.

4   Furthermore, homework is contributing to the obesity problem in United States. We have too many overweight children, and their extra weight is damaging their health. Just like the daughter who didn't have time to play catch, kids are sitting at a desk for hours when they could be exercising.

Name_____ Date_____

5   But isn't homework still a valuable use of time? After all, teachers assign homework to make sure students understand the material. It gives kids the chance to practice academic skills. There's a problem, though. Kids learn through playing just as much they do from homework.

6   Playing is the primary way kids learn about the world. A game of Chinese checkers is a bonding experience for families. But it also teaches kids how to follow rules and how to win and lose respectfully. And it's a real-world opportunity to practice their problem-solving skills. Who needs homework when playing provides many of the same benefits?

7   Some homework is necessary—no matter how young or old the student. Kids need to read regularly. There is no substitute for learning to love reading, and homework is an excellent tool for teaching that. Kids should also be responsible for completing independent projects. Independent projects provide kids with the chance to apply the skills they learn in class.

8   But it's time to say "stop" to mountains of homework for elementary school students. No more worksheets of hundreds of math drills. No more assignments about subjects the teacher didn't even cover in class. And, please, stop assigning so much homework that kids don't have the chance to play outside with their families!

Name_____ Date_____

Close Reading 1: Read for Main Ideas and Details

"Down with Homework!" is mostly about the effects of bringing home too much homework each day. Read the opinion/argument piece and underline the key details that support the main idea. Then complete the graphic organizer using details from the opinion/argument piece. You can add to the graphic organizer if necessary.

Homework

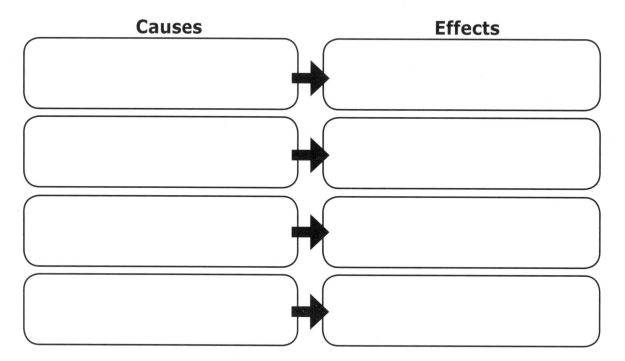

Causes   **Effects**

Collaborative Conversations

Discuss your answers with a partner. When you are the speaker, state your ideas and explain why you think they support the main idea. When you are the listener, ask questions to clarify what the speaker says.

Sentence Frames

Speaker: The author's main point is . . .

I know this because . . .

Listener: What evidence in the text leads you to say that?

What details does the author use to describe that?

Name_____ Date_____

Close Reading 2: Build Vocabulary

Reread the text. Locate each word or phrase, and identify context clues to determine its meaning. Underline the context clues as you read. Share your definitions or meanings with your partner and check your definitions using a dictionary.

Word or Phrase	Context Clues	What the Text Says It Means
assign		
instead		
learn		
opportunity		
independent		

Think-Share-Write

Collaborate with your partner to generate new sentences showing your understanding of each word or phrase. Choose two of the new sentences and write them in the space below.

_____

_____

_____

Name_____ Date_____

Close Reading 3: Identify Text Structure Examples

Part I: Read and Annotate

In this text, the author mainly uses a cause/effect text structure to describe what happens when kids take home too much homework each day. Reread the text and underline examples of this text structure. Be sure to underline any signal words or phrases used by the author that reinforce the author's use of the cause/effect text structure.

Part II: Collaborative Conversations

With a partner, discuss your examples using the following questions.

Discussion Questions	Our Notes
1. What text signal words helped you identify your examples?	
2. Did the author always use signal words? Explain how you were able to identify a cause-and-effect relationship that did not include signal words.	
3. How does a cause/effect text structure help you understand the main idea of this text?	
4. Reread paragraph 1. The author uses descriptive words like *seven hours*, *crispy apple*, and *big pile*, but the text structure is cause/effect. How do these words help you understand the text?	

Part III: Visualize

Draw a picture of what the author wants you to see in paragraphs 3 and 4. Share your drawing with a partner. How are your drawings similar? How are they different?

Name_____ Date_____

Close Reading 4: Build Deeper Understanding

Collaborative Conversations

Reread the text with a partner and discuss the questions. Use information from the text and your annotations to answer the questions. In your discussion, remember to express your ideas clearly and ask questions to better understand each other.

Close Reading Questions	What is the author's purpose for writing this text?	What connection does the author make between homework and obesity?	Does the author want get rid of homework altogether? How do you know?
Text Evidence			
Inference/ Answer			

Name_____ Date_____

Apply Knowledge Through Writing

Part I: Collaborative Conversations

With a partner, read and analyze the prompt. Use the following questions in your discussion.

Writing Prompt

In "Down with Homework!" the author writes about the effects of bringing home too much homework each day. Write a short essay that tells about your experience with homework. Is it similar to or different from the examples in the opinion/argument piece? Support your ideas with information from the text.

Analyze the Prompt	My Thoughts
Is this prompt narrative or informative/explanatory?	
What is it asking me to write about?	
What are my ideas about this prompt?	

Part II: Write

Develop and write a short informative essay. Be sure to . . .

1. state your topic,

2. use details and text evidence to develop the topic,

3. use linking words and phrases,

4. add a concluding sentence.

Sentence Frames

Speaker: A key idea that supports the main idea is . . .

I know this because . . .

Listener: Tell me why you chose this detail . . .

Why did you choose this detail?

Speaker: The main characters are . . .

The main problem in the story is . . .

Listener: What details does the author use to describe this?

What can you tell from that?

Speaker: This detail is important because . . .

Based on the information in the text . . .

Listener: Could you tell me more about that detail?

What details does the author use to describe that?

Speaker: The speaker's main point is . . .

Based on the information in the speech . . .

Listener: What information in the speech leads you to say that?

What details does the speaker use to describe that?

Speaker: This detail makes me think . . .

The author explores the idea that . . .

Listener: Tell me why you chose that detail.

Why did you choose this detail?

Rubrics

Narrative Writing Checklist

	Yes	No	Not Sure
1. My narrative has a strong lead that catches the reader's attention.			
2. I include specific details to establish the time, place, and characters involved.			
3. I use dialogue to develop experiences and events and to show the responses of characters to situations.			
4. I include description to help my readers visualize the events and characters.			
5. I include dialogue or express what people said.			
6. My narrative is logically sequenced.			
7. I use sequence (transitional) words and phrases to manage the sequence of events.			
8. My narrative has a strong ending.			
9. I tell my personal narrative using kid-friendly language.			
10. I use describing words, including adjectives and adverbs, to tell my story.			
11. I use both concrete and sensory language to convey experiences and events precisely.			
12. I provide a conclusion that follows from the experiences and events in my narrative.			

Quality Writing Checklist

I looked for and corrected . . .	Yes	No	Not Sure
sentence fragments and run-ons.			
parts of speech (pronouns, auxiliaries, adjectives, prepositions).			
grammar.			
indented paragraphs.			
punctuation.			
capitalization.			
spelling.			

Rubrics

Informative/Explanatory Writing Checklist

	Yes	No	Not Sure
1. I researched my topic and organized my information into notes that helped me write my text.			
2. I introduce my topic clearly and use words that grab my readers' attention.			
3. I keep my paper organized by grouping information together in a way that makes sense. I use paragraphs and sections.			
4. I use headings to organize my sections.			
5. The information in my report is accurate.			
6. I support my points with facts, definitions, concrete details, and quotations.			
7. I include graphics to support my information.			
8. I include captions that explain each graphic.			
9. I use linking words, signal words, and phrases to link ideas.			
10. My report includes different viewpoints so that I do not sway my readers to think one way.			
11. I include a strong conclusion that keeps my readers thinking.			
12. I choose words that make my text interesting to read and easy to understand. I include words that connect to the topic.			
13. I use at least one primary source.			
14. I use a formal voice.			

Quality Writing Checklist

I looked for and corrected . . .	Yes	No	Not Sure
sentence fragments and run-ons.			
parts of speech (pronouns, auxiliaries, adjectives, prepositions).			
grammar.			
indented paragraphs.			
punctuation.			
capitalization.			
spelling.			

Rubrics

Opinion/Argument Writing Checklist

	Yes	No	Not Sure
1. I introduce my topic with a lead that grabs my readers' attention.			
2. I state my opinion at the beginning of my paper.			
3. I include reasons for my opinion based on my own thoughts about the topic.			
4. I group connected ideas together.			
5. I use evidence from the text to support my opinion.			
6. I use linking words, signal words, and phrases to link ideas.			
7. I include a concluding sentence or paragraph that makes my readers think.			
8. My opinion follows an organized structure.			
9. I choose words that make sense and make my opinion interesting.			
10. I do not change my opinion.			
11. I use different types of sentences.			
12. I use my voice to show people how much I care about my opinion.			

Quality Writing Checklist

I looked for and corrected . . .	Yes	No	Not Sure
sentence fragments and run-ons.			
parts of speech (pronouns, auxiliaries, adjectives, prepositions).			
grammar.			
indented paragraphs.			
punctuation.			
capitalization.			
spelling.			

Notes:

Notes:

_____

_____

_____

_____

_____

_____

_____

_____

_____

_____

_____